MARSH "REGGIE" WHITE

A HUDDLE FOR RIGHTEOUSNESS

Editor: Roxane Christ

authorHOUSE™

1663 LIBERTY DRIVE, SUITE 200
BLOOMINGTON, INDIANA 47403
(800) 839-8640
WWW.AUTHORHOUSE.COM

© 2005 MARSH "REGGIE" WHITE. All Rights Reserved.

No part of this book may be reproduced, stored in a retrieval system, or transmitted by any means without the written permission of the author.

First published by AuthorHouse 03/22/05

ISBN: 1-4208-1587-3 (sc)
ISBN: 1-4208-1586-5 (dj)

Library of Congress Control Number: 2004099380

Printed in the United States of America
Bloomington, Indiana

This book is printed on acid-free paper.

DEDICATION

IN KEEPING WITH THE TRADITION OF:

Jim Elliott
Through Gates of Splendor
Wrestler Martyred in South America

Eric Liddell
Chariots of Fire Best Picture movie
Olympic Gold Medalist Paris-1924 Perished in China

Billy Sunday
Great Evangelist
Baseball Player

It has been written in the memory of and keeping with the tradition of great Christian Athletes who have gone before me and have lived their lives and lost the same to honor our Lord and Savior Jesus Christ.

This book is dedicated to my adoptive mother Irene Holmes with special and undying gratefulness to Roxane Christ my editor.

PROLOGUE

They did not understand him and as a result they began to fear him and his influence on the people. He compared their religious system to worn out garments and old wineskins. The bright light inside of him repelled the darkness and the darkness comprehended it not. He had to go! Every word that he spoke, reached its' target, hit its' mark, and exposed their rotten decaying corpses. He made them very uncomfortable. Jesus knowing this told them a parable that practically guaranteed his death. It was a story of a king who was preparing a wedding feast for his son; his oxen had been butchered and his cows fattened for this special occasion. He sent out slaves with invitations to the locals to come to the feast; but the invitations were spurned, the slaves beaten, and his servants killed by those who were bloodthirsty and had rejected his invitation. Enraged, the King told his servants to go to the highways and into the streets and find both good and evil and bring them to the wedding feast that he had prepared for his son. The banquet hall was filled with guests who were drinking, eating, dancing, and enjoying themselves.

During the feast, as the King was making his rounds in the large hall and greeting the hundreds of guests who had been invited, he came upon a gentleman who was thoroughly enjoying the best tasting steak that he had ever eaten. The juice was dripping from his lips onto his robes as he gorged himself. Right in the middle of a big bite; he felt someone tap him on the shoulder. It was the King. Panic set in because he knew that he had crashed the gate of this party without the proper clothing that had been given to the guests by the King. He was a dead duck.

"Where are your garments for my wedding feast sir?"
The roasted piece of ox stuck between his teeth never made it to his stomach. The King quickly called for the servants to come and throw the gate-crasher outside. Three huge bouncers picked him up by the seat of his pants and the scruff of his collar and threw

him outside on his face. All of the people at the wedding feast who watched this were awfully glad that they had on the right clothing that the King had provided for the wedding feast. The King then turned to his servants and guests and said,
"Many have been called but few have been chosen."[1]

The scribes and Pharisees of Jesus' day considered themselves as a lock in for the wedding feast of the coming kingdom. They had the right pedigree, they lived in the right nation, and they were the called of God. They had everything but the right set of clothes for the wedding feast; and this parable was targeted directly at them and they knew it. Jesus got under their skin, he was not politically correct, and the high priest made a decision that he thought would remedy the situation. Kill him! Is it not better for one man to perish than for a whole nation to be destroyed?

The Huddle for Righteousness is about wearing the proper clothing that God has given to his people. Adam and Eve received these garments after they were kicked out of the garden, Abraham wore them in Canaan, the prodigal son received them when he came home, and the apostle Paul wore them on a daily basis.

The Huddle for Righteousness is the invitation to prepare you for the wedding of the Son of God. Are you wearing the proper garments for the wedding of His son? Jesus Christ has offered us a new set of garments for our old faded blue jeans and sad looking T-shirts. It is this new set of garments that I desire to write about and offer you to try them on as your new suit of clothes. This book gives me the privilege and the joy of inviting you to the wedding feast of the Lamb, it will replenish your soul, it offers you refreshments of good food, a warm soothing bath, fresh new garments of righteousness, a bright shiny new sword for your battle, and a healing balm from Gilead for the wounded heart. **Selah.** Drink deeply my friend.

---

[1] Matt 22:9-14

Chapter One

Three miles from the ends of the earth, you will run across a bump in the road which I call the place of my birth. It is a quiet sleepy little town that few people on earth have ever passed through. It has never been famous or renowned for anything or anyone of great importance. For personal reasons only, I will not reveal its location for this is a very private place that is lost in time. Mulberry is its name and it is a rock and a hard place. This is where I first drew breath from this life. Running through this hamlet is a well worn asphalt road pitted of numerous potholes, on either side of which you will find a grocery store and a gas station. About one mile due north of town and off to the main highway, you will see an old dirt road where the grass still grows high center and scrapes the bottom of your car to this very day. The tires of many vehicles have cut deep ruts that are filled with the red clay dirt, which is common in Mulberry. Your journey will take you pass several corn fields that are occupied by crows and cow birds that follow closely behind farmer Brown's plow looking for insects (or anything that could fill their gizzard). Further down the road you will see another dirt path; this is where you want to take your first right because this is the road that takes you to my childhood home. But first, you will have to negotiate the crossing of a bridge that has been washed out at least four times within the last ten years and nobody knows if it has ever been repaired properly. It can barely support human traffic let alone a vehicle of any sort. Now as you pass over this bridge don't let the car doors, motor parts, skeletons, and tires that you see scattered on the creek's bed concern you in any way. Some have actually made it across this bridge and lived to tell about it, besides life is too short to sweat the small stuff. Round the next corner to your right and from a distance you will be able to see the place where my life was sculpted into an everlasting shape. It is a gray two room never been painted wooden shack with a kitchen at the back and a pot-bellied stove in the middle of it. There was no running water and no electricity but we did have holes in the north wall. When the winter came we were put in a predicament because our front side was fried from getting too close to the pot bellied stove and our back side was frozen from being exposed to the drafty holes in the wall. We got our water from a well dug in the backyard and the stream running down past grandma's house in front of the shack. A huge China Berry tree gave us shade from the blistering sun and a limb around which we threw a rope and swung from it during the summer. Ah! Life was simple and also good.

We were sharecroppers by trade, chopping cotton in the spring and pulling their snow balls in the summer and fall. It was my grandfather's life and my great grandfather's before him, and it has been passed on down to my generation. Life may have been uncomplicated by modern standards but it had been hard in this place. It makes the people who live here a hard people who give birth to children that grow up to be hard. A map will not help you if you are trying to locate this place, for we were considered to be totally insignificant to the powers that be when they drew up their charts. The census takers were of no help either. They kept complaining about having to cross some bridge – especially after they had lost a few cars. From that time on they counted us by word of mouth. About two-hundred and fifty people made a living from this red clay, (if you throw in a few dogs and cats roaming the place; even they are threatening to leave because of the relentless heat and too few rats to sate their hunger). The last we saw of the field mice was when they were picketing our house because of the lack of food in the corn fields. Food was scarce for us as well. If Daddy didn't find any rabbits in the woods or if the crops failed because of the droughts we were down to sugar water and bread. As a family we fared little better than the animals we were trying to raise and the crops we were attempting to grow. Living there made you like a root out of dry ground.

So why do I miss it? I don't know; the only thing that this place gave me as a boy growing up was hard work, sweat and tears but I would give my eye teeth to be back there.

Destiny has a way of giving with the right hand and taking away with the left. It can be both cruel and kind to a small country boy who cannot see the end of a long dirt road. The cruelty is needed to break strong proud backs and the kindness is needed to give the encouragement to see the end of the road. If this place could be tasted the traveler would say that Mulberry is bittersweet. The sweetness was a cocoon that protected the young and somewhat innocent. (I don't dare say completely innocent or else every mother on the face of the earth will call me something that I can't put in print as of yet.) But life is sweet in the country because you have time to appreciate your surroundings and to open your heart to close relationships, which is a great formula for growth and development in a lot of areas of your life. Life slows down in Mulberry and waits for you to catch up. Of course in this place it is like in any place else; some of us were like porcupines, we had our fine points but we were not easily approached – that would be me by the way.

Grandma lived just up the road from me a good three hundred yards over the Bermuda grass and sandy dirt that was covered with tire tracks. Whenever she had fixed too much breakfast she would call for one of us to come and help her finish off the biscuits and gravy. I remember running down to her house until my four year old toes would burn on the hot sand on the road and I would quickly run back onto the cool Bermuda grass to cool off.

Life slowed down to a crawl then and sometimes it even appeared to stop. Life was good in Mulberry; I just did not know it at the time.

The 'bitter' of the bittersweet, comes on the day you have to up and leave your cocoon and that is when all hell breaks loose. Country folks and city slickers do have much in common except eating, sleeping, and talking about the weather. If you go beyond that the communication gets a bit complicated. I had never met people outside of my family. I had been around Curtis, Bang, Ronnie, and Stanley all my life but outside of that circle, my exposure to people had been limited to say the least. If you asked me why we called my cousin 'Bang' the only response you would receive from me, is a blank stare and an 'I don't know'. As far as I can tell somebody had a little too much moonshine when they were passing out names to people; and if you mixed it up with some white lightening, things can get really strange.

Then one day in Mulberry an event occurred that changed the course of my entire life. I had no earthly idea of what was about to happen to me. It was a day that I will never forget for as long as I live. This one single event left a scar on my soul that I can't erase. Whenever, I think of this, it is like scraping my fingernails down the side of a blackboard. Mrs. McIntire whom I met on this eventful day of my life was an extremely beautiful woman with long black hair and one of the sweetest dispositions that I have ever known. On this occasion she became an unsolicited witness to the trauma this young country boy was experiencing. Most of the kids responded to her very well as she showed everyone to their desk and to their rooms. But not me! I wasn't used to being surrounded by four large walls for eight hours a day. Oh, the fear that could be seen in my eyes they looked like silver dollars and there was no place to run. Home was 25 miles away by bus. And here I was sitting among all of these six year old 'Martians' who were eating crackers and waiting to take me captive back to Mars and wondering what the fuss was all about. So I let out the biggest scream that's ever been heard this side of heaven. It sounded a lot like hog-killing time back home. I rushed over to where my friend Bang was sitting quietly by this time and he couldn't decide if he wanted to run from me or hit me in the mouth in order to stop the weeping, wailing, and gnashing of teeth. First grade was absolute murder for me and Mrs. McIntire.

Finally I couldn't take it any more. I ran out of the classroom to find my Aunt Ruby who was in high school at the time. When I walked into her classroom the teacher looked at me with the same look that you give to house guest who has worn out the welcome mat. It was a look that said, "If you *ever* come to this classroom again, I will ring your neck until your eyeballs pop out" – kind of look.

"Little boy, this is the 302nd time that you have come to this classroom. You can't come here anymore."

I remember thinking, "Shoot me, somebody please shoot me and relieve me of this misery." The separation from home, family, and close relationships was the most painful event of my young life. And so from that time on whenever I escaped from my penitentiary on leave to go and see my aunt, I would stay in the hall way leaning against the walls near the door of the class and making sure that the hatchet lady didn't see me, just to be near my aunt.

Seven thousand years ago there was a man who also lived in a cocoon. In a perfect environment, he prospered and matured as he walked with God. Time stood still back then as you had time to forge quality relationships. In this environment he was protected mentally, physically, and emotionally. The sun would always shine and the rain would come down only when the plants needed it. The weather was always a perfect 70° Fahrenheit. There was never any harsh winter or cold weather. It was paradise on earth and a perfect place. In the perfectly blue skies that was a protective layer that surrounded the earth and kept the sun from harming the atmosphere and the people in it. The people who lived in this environment ate nothing but vegetables and fruit no animal had to be killed or slain for meat. The trees that they ate from were always in bloom and always yielded various fruits without end. If at any time there was a lack of nourishment in their bodies they knew exactly where to go and what to eat. Plants and trees provided a source of healing if healing was needed.[2] The colorful and bright serpents that were in the garden had a very specific purpose. They didn't hiss and spit as much as they do today. They were there to maintain Adam's health and if he needed assistance in the area of his body, their flickering tongues

---

[2] Revelation 22:2

would search his body to find the ailment and would envenom him with the proper dosage for healing. All of the animals were there for the purpose of helping Adam to keep God's edict of being fruitful and filling the earth. Ahh! Life was good!

Life was extremely good. But the best part about living in this place was that you could have an uninterrupted walk with God. He actually looked forward to seeing and being with you every day. Now as you would have it, not everyone was happy about Adam living in a perfect environment and being one of the untouchables. Sinister and evil eyes began to study his every move, listen to his every word, and watch his every mood looking for weak spots in this perfect man but could find none. So, the evil one bided his time tapped his fingers and waited for the opportune moment. He and his followers had just recently been kicked out of heaven and they had been looking for a rebound, a place to start over and he had set his sights on earth and on Adam. Adam seemed to be the perfect target seeing that his attempt at a coupe in heaven had failed miserably. He desperately needed a Kingdom, a place to rule. Many of his subjects had been cast into prison and were sentenced to thousands of years in chains, and he needed a victory, a notch in his belt. He was still smarting from the beating he took when he had tried to take over God's realms.

However, there was a powerful stronghold of protection around the man in the garden. God had placed around him a fortress that guarded his thoughts and the source of his thoughts. None of his words were contaminated by evil in any way, shape or form. The well from which he drew his thoughts was deep and pure; Adam enjoyed drinking from it every day because that's where he communed with God.

The enemy lurked in the shadows and behind the bushes scheming, planning, and plotting his next move. He knew that the key to gaining control of Adam and of his Kingdom was to control and contaminate the source of his thinking and to pollute his well. He had to break the barrier; but how? The protection that covered his mind and soul had to be breached. "What should I do?" He pondered and pondered. God was too strong as was the case when he tried to take over the Kingdom of heaven; and his protection around Adam was too complete. Then one day he carefully watched how Adam named every animal that God had brought to him. He saw how Adam knew every detail about them demonstrating his utter brilliance. His combination of genius and perfection in all that he did was potentially lethal to Satan and his demons. They needed territory. They needed a Kingdom. They wanted a place to rule. If this man that God had created became fruitful and multiplied as God commanded, the enemy would run into this problem in every nation on the face of the earth. Adam had to be stopped immediately if not sooner. Yet, how do you trap a perfect man?

One of the most evil strategies of the enemy is to take advantage of his victims in the areas of their most basic needs. His diligent observation of Adam as he had named each animal would possibly give him an opening. He also knew that God had brought the animals before Adam for a specific purpose and that was to expose his need for a companion. Ahh! This was it! His patience had finally paid off. Adam noticed that each animal fulfilled a basic need in the other and that without the other there was a lack. The evil genius picked up on it and waited for the opportune moment to spring his trap.

As soon as Adam began to recognize that there was something missing the word came from God,

"It is not good for man to be alone. I will make a helper that is suitable for him."

Would Adam's enemy be so cruel as to use his own basic needs against him? A plan was forming. An evil, rotten, brilliant plan was taking shape in the heart of the enemy. In order for it to work he simply needed to wait for all the right pieces to fall into place. Adam was put into a deep sleep and the Lord God took a rib from him and fashioned the most beautiful being of his creation: a woman. She was perfect in mind, body, and soul and would make a wonderful helper for Adam because she was of a like kind. The enemy then stealthily moved in to observe her close at hand. When Adam first saw her he shouted, "This now at last." He knew he needed a woman, neither a hippo nor a chimp (they were too noisy), not an elephant – too big for his house, nor a dog, because they always left spots on the rug.

Yes, indeed he needed a woman! Something that was taken from him that would complement him. And so God gave him a woman, someone who completed his life. The enemy began to study her in detail as she interacted with Adam. He noticed that even though she was perfect she did not know the animals as well as Adam did nor was she created to do so. Could this loop-hole be exploited he wondered? Thus, he chose a creature that was particularly appealing to Eve and plan 'B' was put into action. There was no small fuss from the serpent that Satan wanted to use because Satan wanted to borrow his suit of clothes for the day. How would you like it if someone crawled into your skin and used your voice and your body?

Since Adam knew the animals down to the last detail, he would surely suspect a serpent that talked to him, especially if he tried to play the "go ahead and eat the apple it's no big deal trick". That was not going to work with Adam but possibly it could work with Eve who did not know the animals the way Adam did and only having received the command not to eat from the tree of knowledge from Adam and not from God. So Satan took on the form of the reluctant serpent in the garden and for the first time an animal spoke. By the way, Balaam's donkey never forgave that serpent for taking first place in the animal speaking contest. This serpent was so charming by nature and so beautifully enticing that Eve was taken in by its approach and looks. She was captivated and completely deceived even in her perfect state. She responded to the serpent's question about the tree in the garden from which she had been forbidden to eat the fruit. Eve's answers gave the serpent encouragement to open the trap door a bit wider. He had successfully separated her from her covering in Adam and now he was peeling back the layers.

But how could something so charming and so beautiful be so deadly in its impact? The serpent's ticket to get Adam to fall was to get part of his rib to do the job for him.

In the end, Eve was deceived but Adam sinned willfully. Adam's sin was a capital offense. It brought death to an entire Kingdom of people and all of Adam's descendants after him. The enemy now had the Kingdom that he had so long desired. Humpty Dumpty was now off his wall, he had suffered a great fall, and none of the King's horses and none of the King's men could put Humpty Dumpty back together again.

The owners of this beautiful paradise knew that the world around them had just been changed from bright yellows and greens to a dark gray and black, for just moments ago they could stand before each other butt naked and know no guilt or shame. They could be completely honest and open with each other without the other getting hurt. A moment ago Adam knew Eve like the back of his hand but now his language was harsh and his behavior towards her was cold and hard. A moment ago they could stand before a Holy God without fear, but now things would be different.

All of a sudden they heard footsteps coming in their direction in the garden and a familiar voice calling out to them,
"Adam! Adam where are you?"
Adam was riddled with guilt and fear and said nothing. These emotions are all new to him. He has never felt fear or guilt before that moment and he had no idea of what was happening to him. His soul was exposed in such a way as to show his true nakedness before God. Living in the garden suddenly became bittersweet. It was a blessing and a curse. His environment of love and protection had been ripped from him and now he stood before a Holy God who had little choice but to judge him. Adam and Eve finally emerged from behind their trees their body covered with fig leaves, their mind in torment and their face rueful and anxious.
"I was naked so I hid myself in the trees when I heard you coming."
"Adam, who told you that you were naked; have you eaten of the tree that was forbidden to you?"
At this point Adam knew that all the wheels had come off and he began to do what every child does when he is caught with his hands in the cookie jar. He lied and then blamed someone else for his misdeed. Inside he is humiliated; he is not only a stranger to God now but also a stranger to his wife. They would have to get to

know one another all over again through a sin contaminated soul. The words that he once used to bless her had changed into sharp piercing daggers that ravaged her heart. The damage that was once kept at a distance was now part of everyday living and reality. Their physical nakedness in the garden that had once represented their spiritual nakedness before God and each other had all been covered with shame before Him. They could no longer afford to be open and honest with each other and before their God. Their mind, soul, and body were screaming for the righteousness they once knew. The very presence of God was a judgment for them and they felt very uncomfortable in his presence. The penetrating eyes of God touched the souls of His creation and nothing was hidden from His sight.

So He left them temporarily and brought them back a covering for their nakedness and he told them, "Because you have done this you will surely die."

After they are sentenced for their capital offense, God kicked them out of the garden.

The trinity then met in counsel; they had to make a decision concerning Adam's future and the future of his descendants.

"Man has become like one of us, knowing good and evil. What shall we do? The plans for paradise on earth will have to be postponed until later; and in order for us to restore paradise, it will cost dearly. In order for us to restore man and paradise one of us must become a man and go to the earth in order to redeem both man and creation"

Chapter Two

The standard for redemption before God is perfection and a life for a life. Adam and his descendents cannot measure up to the standards given by God. A perfect sacrifice is needed, a perfect life must be lived, and a perfect substitute must be provided to pay for the sin of Adam. There is only one standard that God accepts and this standard is perfection.

In order for man to get to heaven he must be as good as God and that was no longer possible through Adam and his descendants. God was facing a dilemma that only He could resolve.

God must someway, somehow impart to man the divine nature[3] or when Adam's descendants go before him they would feel the same fear and shame that Adam and Eve felt when they sinned. His only option in the redemption of man was to give him a nature that was not subject to judgment.

"I will go," Jesus said. "I will go and become one of them. I will go and fight the fight face to face with the same person that Adam lost the kingdom to and I will win the battle to restore man back to us on his terms. I will fight Satan on his own turf as a perfect man and do what Adam should have done in his war against him, and then, I will lay down my life as a sacrifice so that man can live and all of creation can be restored and redeemed."

God the Father spoke up and said,
"The sin of Adam has cost us dearly, he has left us no choice in the sacrifice that we must make to redeem him – a perfect sacrifice is the price to be paid for redemption."

Adam shuffled his feet and finally began to realize the gravity of his sin and how much it would cost God and man. He would now

---

[3] 2Peter 1:4

have to make a living at the sweat of his brow and Eve would have problems giving birth and raising her children. As for the serpent, he didn't want any part of this anymore – too messy of a deal... So he made his way very quickly toward the gates and was looking for a fast way out when God stopped him and told him that his head would be crushed by the seed of the woman one day and that he would crawl on his belly for the rest of his days. Let me tell you the serpent was none to happy about his partnership with Satan; as a matter of fact he was downright put off and he has been hissing and biting folks ever since.

Soon after they left the garden Eve began to bear children. She named the first one Cain who became a tiller of the soil, a farmer. She was plenty excited thinking that this one was the seed that God had promised who would destroy the serpent. But that was not exactly what Cain had in mind when he grew up and his brother came along. It seemed as if he got into a big squabble over his offering with God. God didn't like it but Cain thought it was wonderful. Soon after this encounter, he began to pout, and then he began to stew until he could no longer take the jealousy and he took his knife and slit his brother's throat.

"Okay, God, you want a righteous sacrifice," he shouted angrily. "Here is one for you, I give you my brother. I will offer him up to you as a righteous sacrifice since you preferred his sacrifice over mine. Take him."

Cain was absolutely livid with God. The way that he had cut Abel's throat was the same way that Abel had killed his lamb and offered him up before God. It was an act of utter defiance against God and anger against his brother. He had really been upset ever since God had rejected his offering, and this was his way of taking it out on God. This was not just an overnight occurrence, Cain had been doing his thing and going his own way for quite some time now and this was just the culmination of a series of rebellions. Behind the scenes God's archenemy had convinced Cain not to make his sacrifice an act of faith but rather to just go and do his duty so that he could quickly go his own way and get back to business. Abel's sacrifice was one of faith but Cain simply wanted to perform a duty. When they came to make their offerings before God, God did not even look in Cain's direction. At no time did He acknowledge what Cain had brought to Him but when it came to Abel's sacrifice they were always received with God's commendation and smile. Cain didn't understand this apparent inequity in God's judgment; quickly an argument ensued.

"I worked just as hard as he did to bring my sacrifice. Why am I being rejected?"
"Cain, if you do right, your face will show the condition of your heart; I have given you all the instructions that you need to bring your sacrifice before me in the proper way and to have it be acceptable."

In fact, before God ever looked at Cain and Abel's sacrifices, He had looked inside of their hearts, and found that Cain's heart was not right before him; so as a result his sacrifice was not right before God. Cain's pouting turned into an angry scowl. He left the presence of God in a huff and with the warnings of God still ringing in his ear. God's heart was in pain when Cain demonstrated this kind of behavior because he knew what was coming. He wanted so much for Cain to be right with Him, but He had given Cain the awesome power of choice which could tie the hands of God even though He was omnipotent. What was anger quickly turned into rage which soon gave way to wrath – uncontrollable ire. And when Cain spotted his rival in the field alone, the righteous seed was slaughtered and the hope of man was cut off once again. Even the very first family and the very first thing that man created had problems – the first member of the family turned out to be a murderer.

The prophets tell us that the eyes of the Lord then, moved to and fro throughout the world looking for someone whose heart was completely His, and soon after the murder of Abel, His eyes stopped in a place known as Ur, Ur of Chaldea. There was a man who lived here with his father by the name of Abraham and God's eyes had stopped on him. Abraham heard a voice that he had never heard before telling him to leave Ur and go to a different land that he would show him later.

But Abraham was a bit hard of hearing. On the journey on which God told him to travel, Abraham brought along his father and sister, although God had specifically called upon Abraham and not upon his family. But He is used to people bringing extra baggage and luggage that they do not need to accomplish His will in their lives. Sometimes your kinfolk don't always understand the call on your life and God has to step in and make things clear. Abraham's father got as far as Haran and decided that it looked like a really good place to raise a family and settle down. There was plenty of good farmland for his cattle and plenty of water to raise his sheep, so they pitched their tent in Haran. Big problem! God did not call upon Terah, he had called upon Abraham, and He did not want the family living in Haran, He wanted them to go to Canaan. After Terah's funeral, Abraham decided that maybe God was downright serious about this Canaan thing, so he packed his bags and left for a place that was totally unknown to him.

Now Sarah was not as adventurous as her husband and she let him know that she wasn't exactly crazy about being dragged to the ends of the earth and that they needed to find someplace and to settle down.

"Where are we going Abraham?" There was no response. This caused quite a bit of concern. If she was going to pull up stakes she thought that she should, at least, know where she was headed. There was still no response from Abraham. Then she thought, "My Lord is not only blind, he is also deaf." She'd never been farther than a couple of hundred miles from Ur but now, it sure looked like she was on her way to see places she had never been before. Seeing that her only source of support and opposing vote was six feet under, she finally gave in to the idea. Lot, her nephew, was just as lost as she was but was just happy to be along for the trip. The tall ghostly tales about men being giants in the land of Canaan did not

A HUDDLE FOR RIGHTEOUSNESS

bother him much however. Whenever they did find a place to camp overnight, the servants reminded Abraham that they didn't want to repeat the Haran experience. They could still hear the last words of Terah when he mumbled something Abraham not letting the grass grow under his feet. Whoever this God was that was speaking to Abraham was no joke, and He appeared to be playing for keeps. So they were excited about getting to Canaan.

Then one night just as they had set foot in Canaan, it happened. On a bright starry night with a full moon God took His man outside after a long day with tired muscles and sore feet and told him to look up. And when he did God made a covenant with him. And Abraham gazed at thirty million bright shiny stars when he heard God say,

"Abraham, I will make your descendants as the stars of the sky and I will make of you a great nation."

Abraham knew then that his journey was worth the pain. And when he realized that God had kept His promise – he believed in Him; and God credited that belief to him as righteousness. The burden on Abraham's back just got a little bit lighter. The blueprint was being laid for every generation to follow. Not only was the blueprint for a nation being laid, but also the blueprint for all people of faith and for anyone who desired to be righteous before God.

Abraham thought in his heart, "How can I be declared righteous before God? Shouldn't he demand something of me for his favor? This God is different from any other that I have ever known."

Then he looked up into the skies and smiled again thinking in his heart, "If my descendants are going to be like the stars, Sarah and I are going to be busy for quite some time to come!"

The gods that he knew in Ur of Chaldea demanded services for favor and righteous acts. They demanded purity and holiness and cleansing to be made right before them, but this God was different.

"Why would a God like this bless me and give me a posterity that will reach unto the end of the earth when I have been involved in idol worship all of my life? It appears as though His gifts were unattached. I knew that in my search, somewhere there had to be a God like this."

Now Sarah and Lot went outside of the tent to take in the night air and became a bit concerned when they saw Abraham with his nose in the dirt and his rear end sticking up. This was the posture given to the gods of the Chaldeans right before you sacrificed the fruit of your body for the sins of your soul, but this time Abraham had no sacrifice to offer his God. He was simply lying before God in worship and muttering prayers of thanksgiving. This God that had led him to Canaan was different from the others that were made of wood and stone. Abraham came back to the tent where he found Sarah and Lot staring at him blankly and uncomprehending when they saw the biggest smile that they had ever seen crossing Abraham's face.

"What is it Abraham?" Sarah asked.

He sat down and began to explain to Sarah what had just taken place now that they were in Canaan. Sarah's heart sank because she was afraid to tell Abraham that she was barren; even before they had left Ur she had had her suspicions.

So the promise was of no great matter to Sarah as later on she would laugh at it. But Abraham kept talking about his encounter with God from morning to night. It had really made an impact on his life and he believed it. Finally as they were discussing it over a meal of goat stew Sarah burst into tears. She could not hide the truth from her husband any longer. Abraham needed to know that she could not have any children and that she could not conceive and in the midst of a flood of tears she finally blurted out the truth. Abraham was devastated! How could the promise that God had given to him be fulfilled through a barren woman? Not only was this a shame for Sarah but it was of great embarrassment for Abraham. It was a blow to his masculinity and his prowess as a man. Whenever he passed by his men they gave him the "what's the matter with you?" kind of look. Nevertheless, he decided to gather himself and believe in his God and his faith never wavered and he bore his humility well.

Years had passed until one day Abraham at 80 years of age saw some men walking towards him on the golden horizon in Canaan. The closer they got the more his heart pounded for at eighty years of age he didn't know if he was ready to take on any of his enemies barehanded. He sighed deeply with relief when he found out that it was his old friend that he had met back in Ur. During his stay God reminded him once again of His promise, that Sarah his barren wife would have a child even in her old age. Another 10 years went by and God stopped by to remind Abraham again that His promises were good. Now the Lord didn't exactly wear out the welcome mat but these visits were to let Abraham know that His promises were good and that He intended to keep them.

Finally when he was 100 years old and Sarah was 90, Abraham saw his old friend in the distance and he rushes to get his camp in order to receive him. Abraham had aged but his friend looked much the same as he did in their initial meeting years ago. Greetings were exchanged and then there was silence until God gazed into his eyes to make his announcement,

"Abraham, your wife will be pregnant and by this time next year you will have that son that I have promised to you."

Abraham thought it over and gazed back into God's eyes and began to laugh with God's approval. God realized that Abraham had finally gotten his point and he laughed with him. Abraham was in hysterics as the whole camp came to see why the loud laughter. He knew that God was good at keeping His promises and the entire camp heard him burst out in laughter. Now Sarah was inside the tent and overhears the remark and begins to remind herself of her barren condition. She laughed inside but there was no evidence on her face or her lips.

"Fat chance! Abraham is dead and I am old. This is not going to happen. We stopped trying twenty years ago when the brook dried up."

She stuck her head through the tent flap with a smirk on her face, just in time to hear God asking her why she laughed. She was stunned – how did He know? No one had heard her laugh but she had been caught red handed. She stuttered as she blurted out the quickest and best lie that came to her mind and very quickly retreated back into the tent after she said,

"Not me, I didn't laugh Lord!"

It would seem that Adam and Sarah were suffering from the same disease. One tried to hide from an omnipresent God who made the trees behind which he was hiding, and the other tried to lie to an omniscient God who gave her the tongue and the mind to lie. Sad sacks the both of them.

Earlier Sarah had asked Abraham to go in to Hagar the Egyptian handmaid so that they could have a son and fulfill God's promise. Hagar did conceive and gave them a son, Ishmael, but he was not the son of the promise. Sarah had gotten desperate and Abraham was confused so they hatched a scheme to fulfill what only God could do. It never occurred to Sarah that her barrenness would be a showcase for the miraculous power of God. She never realized that this was by God's design and that he was going to use her barrenness to bring him honor and glory and that it would be proof that this child was the handiwork of God alone. The seed of righteousness has to be brought forth by God.

God was in the process of putting Humpty Dumpty back together again when it became quite obvious that there was one piece of Humpty that was still missing after the debacle with Hagar, Sarah, and Abraham. After His next act however, what God was after and what He desired from Abraham and his descendants, would become abundantly clear. Not only would God be honored by this but also Abraham's honor and masculinity would be affirmed when he walked among the men even at a hundred although he had little to do with the conception or birth of Isaac. None of his men would be able to do what he did when they reached a hundred. Now when he walked among the men he could give them that 'I've still got it' look.

It is a wonderful story wrapped in a mystery that God was weaving in through Abraham and his descendants. The story had begun with Adam and Eve and it was now making its way down throughout the ages and like any good story it has its own plot and plans that go arwy but God had always been able to keep His main characters and plots on center stage. Abraham was now the main character in this epic and it was time for a tremendous drama and tragedy to unfold in his life.

Abraham was about to be put through a tremendous test of faith. It would change his life forever along with the way he lived and worshipped God. God does not view mistakes and hardships the way we do. He has no downside to him. Therefore, every event that comes the way of his people He uses as a teaching opportunity or an object lesson. Nothing is wasted in the maturing of his children. And so it was with Abraham.

One day as Abraham was sitting by the campfire wondering what he would have for his next meal, God spoke to him and said, *"Abraham!"*

"Here I am, Lord!"

"Abraham, I want you to take your son who you love very much and go to the land of Moriah and offer him as a sacrifice to me."

Abraham pondered the request made by God; "Didn't I just get through waiting over thirty years for a son? Why would He take him away? Is this the same God that brought me out of Ur? Could this be the same God who gave me all of those promises and now it appears that He is backing down on them? How can this be?" Although these thoughts were still present in his mind after he packed his bags and kissed Sarah goodbye; he headed off to Moriah without hesitation. It was a long journey, but at the foot of the mountains he told his servants to wait there and then he said something that became typical of the friend of God. He told his servants that he and the boy would return from their trip up the mountains. How could this be? Didn't God give him a direct command? And wasn't there a large knife strapped to his side? How could he talk about Isaac returning with him when he was to be sacrificed?

Along the way Abraham had put two-and-two-together. He knew that God was not one to tell lies. He also knew that God had given him a promise that his seed would be as the stars in the heavens and that his descendants would come through Isaac and no other. So if God wanted Isaac to be his sacrifice that meant that he would also raise him up from the grave. Abraham's faith in God grew stronger and not weaker as a result of this test of faith.

Now Isaac began to be a bit concerned when Abraham put some wood on his back and began sharpening this knife. There were no goats or sheep around for him to sacrifice so where would he get the sacrifice? As they finally climbed to the top of the mountain Isaac pops the question, "Father, I see the wood and the altar, but where is the sacrifice?"

There was a look in his eye that was asking Abraham, "Are you really going to do what I think you are going to do? Why would you do this to your own son?"

Now God is watching Abraham and heard him say; "son, God will provide for himself a sacrifice."

Abraham did not completely understand God's request either, but he did understand what it meant to place his faith in God. This is what God treasured most in Abraham; his absolute trust in Him. The knife was drawn from his side as Abraham lifted the chin of Isaac in order to locate the jugular vein, and on its way down the angel of the Lord caught his right hand by the wrist in midair.

"Abraham," this powerful voice shook the earth beneath him when the angel spoke. *"Do not harm your son. Look behind you, God has provided a sacrifice for himself."*

And there in the thicket a male ram had his horns caught between the long briars there on the mountain. Abraham took the ram that he did not see on his way up and slaughtered him. This time the knife went straight across the jugular vein as a grateful father and his son watched an innocent ram gasping for his last breath of air.

On the way home, Isaac began to question his father about why God had asked him to be sacrificed and his father's reply was classic. He knew that some day in the future, God would provide a permanent sacrifice for himself and he also knew that his descendants would not need to offer sacrifices unto God, either human or fleshly acts or deeds. He told Isaac of how he and Sarah had good intentions in trying to do God's work and trying to help God to fulfill his own promises. They had neither the power nor the authority to do so, but it sure made a mess of things.

"Remember, my son, the works of God and the works of men may not always be the same thing; sometimes they are like oil and water, they do not mix."

Isaac looked at him as he said, "Father, are you telling me that the birth of Ishmael was a mistake?"

Abraham loved his son Ishmael but began to recall how he constantly had fought with Isaac and how Hagar was constantly bickering with Sarah. Was Ishmael a mistake in human judgment? Was he a constant example of what happens when men try to do the work of God without waiting on him even if the wait is over thirty years? Abraham looked at Isaac and said,

"You will always have trouble with Ishmael, yes, you my son and all of your descendants for as long as there is life on this earth."

His eyes told Isaac the story that even though he loved Ishmael he had to send him away. He also knew that his decision to have Ishmael was not unlike the decision that Adam made in the garden that caused the fall of all of creation. They had gotten it wrong with Hagar, and his following the beliefs and customs of his culture did not hold sway with God and in walking with him. The long walk home was a joyous one even after the tremendous test of faith that both men had to endure.

When a tired and hungry Abraham came back home to Sarah and a warm bed and hot meals that had already been prepared for him he began to meditate. God quietly spoke to his heart and said,

"Abraham, you could not have a baby, and I gave you a baby, you could not have descendants and I gave you descendants, you did not have to sacrifice your son, I gave you a ram to sacrifice. Abraham, know that the work before me that you must do has already been done for you."

A smile came over Abraham's face when he heard this as he rested and then he slept.

Chapter Three

Now one of Abraham's descendants found out the hard way that a righteous life is not something man can easily attain. He too like Abraham knew that God was at work in his life. So much so that in order to fulfill his mission he killed a man. He had decided to use his great skills as a leader of men and thinking that this would work with God's people, he tried the same strategy. It failed miserably! No one followed him, even though a year before he had led great armies throughout Africa while conquering entire nations. He was feared and respected but not before God. He fell flat on his face and had to learn to walk all over again. So, God took him aside for forty long years to train and re-train him to listen to his voice and to do his will. Many people today much like this great soldier have claimed to have heard the voice of God when it was nothing more but gas in their stomach. And when the gas was passed so were they.

God really doesn't get too awfully excited about those kinds of people except when they start telling lies in his name then He says that you should leave them under a pile of rocks and have long talks with any more (wannabe prophets) who have heard from God.

So how do you know if you have heard from God? How do we know God's voice when he has spoken? There are so many voices that speak and claim to be the voice of God leading people down the wrong paths and to destruction and they all claim to have heard from God. It is interesting that Abraham heard from God directly and not through a mediator. He had his most difficult trials when he listened to the voice of others and not from God. In the eastern culture to hear from God does not necessarily mean that you need a mediator. God spoke directly to the men of old and they knew that it was God speaking.

In the eastern culture to hear and to obey was much the same thing. They are not two different entities. They enjoyed a first hand relationship with God that needed no intervention from man or priest, and when God spoke there was no second-guessing or scratching of the head. They simply did it. King Saul had heard the word of God directly from Samuel and he said; "Yes Lord". God had told him to kill off all of the Amalekites when he came upon them and not to spare one soul. And so on his return trip he ran into the prophet Samuel. This spoiled everything, because when he came upon the Amalekite some of the spoils began to look pretty good to him and the word that God had given him earlier somehow got lost in the shuffle.

"Hello, Samuel! We have carried out the commands of the Lord."

Saul knew that he had been caught red-handed but he cleverly covered himself and wanted to carry Samuel along with his masquerade. The prophet of God saw right through what Saul was trying to do and rebuked him strongly.

"Saul, if you have obeyed the voice of the Lord then why do I hear the sound of cattle and see the King still alive?"

Saul did not know whether to spit or whistle. He stuttered and he stammered and then the lie came out. He had not obeyed the voice of the Lord because he had never heard him. Obedience and hearing are the same. God had told him to kill everything but what Saul heard was that you should kill everything except for the King and some of the spoils. The wax that had clogged up Saul's ears had made its way to his brain because to hear God's voice and not obey is not to hear at all. Hearing God speak is not a physical matter. People who have perfect hearing have never heard God. Hearing God speak is not a matter of having the physical ability to hear, it is a matter of a heart that is open before God. Saul's heart was not right before God and as a result the hardness of his soul and the stone that was in his heart moved up about 18 inches.

Finally, Isaac began to comprehend why Abraham could obey God when he told him to make the sacrifice and why he could tell his men that he was going to return with his son in three days. Because the moment when Abraham took his first step towards the land of Moriah God began to give him insight and knowledge. It was when he finally left Haran that God gave him knowledge of his plans for the future and made an unconditional covenant with him. Therefore knowledge in the spiritual realm is not all about the gathering of facts, intelligence, skills, and study. Knowledge in the spiritual realm is hearing and obeying the voice of God. Somewhere en route to Moriah when Abraham's obedience was complete God revealed to him that he would bring his son back alive.

The priest who carried the Ark of the Covenant discovered that obedience is knowledge when they came to the Jordan River and the water was a swift running current. They were caught between a rock and a hard place because they knew that they were the only ones allowed to carry the Ark. God told them to go forward into the Jordan River. Now, there was a bit of a concerned look on their faces. They didn't mind moving forward and sticking their twinkly little toes in the water but at midstream; it could be a bit deep and the Ark was more than heavy. It was not going to float but rather it would take a few priests down with it. Well, the first sacrifice, I mean priest, stuck his toe in the water as if he was testing the temperature of his bath water. And lo and behold when they all went into the Jordan the river dried up. Knowledge came after obedience. They would still be waiting to cross the Jordan River to this day if they had never obeyed.

The psalmist wrote of how he had learned to hear the voice of God and obey: and how he waited patiently for the moving of the Lord and to hear his voice. It didn't come easy for him. He had fallen into the deep dark pits that hunters had set to trap dangerous animals and the Lord had saved him from certain destruction when he heard his cry; and how he had fallen into the deadly quicksand with no one around to save him and the Lord had pulled him out of the miry clay and placed his feet on solid rock. It had taught him a new song to sing and a new hymn of praise born out of his experiences with God.

His songs spoke of the happiness found in those who trusted in the Lord and who put away their false idols for the living God. When he went to the temple to pray it came from a heart that knew his God.

O' Lord, you have done many things for us, O Lord our God: there is none like you! You have made many wonderful plans for us. I could never speak of them all—their number is so great! But born out of the psalmist experience with God was his knowledge that God does not require sacrifices of any kind[4] from men or the sons of men. Instead of sacrifices my Lord of bulls, goats, and human service, you have given me ears to hear you speak directly to my heart. You have given me a first hand relationship with you, because you have put your laws in my heart, and I am able to listen to your Holy Spirit speaking directly to my heart. O Lord my ears were clotted with the debris of religion and human efforts to do your will, this idolatry kept you from speaking directly to me but now you have unclogged my ears and given me new ears to hear you. I hear you speaking clearly when you tell me that no human sacrifice (as you demonstrated with Abraham and Isaac on Moriah) or service is needed to please. Lord if you needed money you could sell the cattle on a thousand hills and the hills themselves, if money was an issue, for they all belong to you. Lord if you needed worshipped the millions of saints and angels that surround you are more qualified to worship you than any man or woman here on earth. The cherubim's that surround you day and night call out to you holy, holy, holy give you a depth of worship that we could never imagine. If I sell all of my possessions and head out to the ends of the earth and sacrifice my life for you, it does not gain your favor, if I offer my body as a sacrifice even as Isaac did on Moriah, it would not cause your face to shine upon me. Lord, the sacrifices of men are not what you desire nor are they what you need. Therefore O, Lord my God, I will walk before you in the righteousness that you have provided for me and by your Holy Spirit that lives in me for I have realized that I cannot keep your law and live by your commandments. If I try and keep your commandments, the darkness will overtake me and seize the opportunity to make my

---

[4] Psalm 40:6

life displeasing to you. I am but flesh and blood Lord; my spirit is willing but my flesh is too weak and this you know. Lord, you have provided something else to keep your standards and laws for me and provide for you the sacrifice and offerings that you require.[5] Selah.

As the psalmist began to reflect on his life his mind took him back to the stresses and strains of his life under the laws of Moses. The law and the legalistic system was not only unsuccessful in what it attempted to do; it had kept him from experiencing the goodness of God and the righteous life. Everything that he had attempted to do in his spiritual life had failed. His heart was sincere and his love for God was certain, but what was causing all of this failure in his spiritual life? The goodness of his heart was evident, but living out those good intentions were only met with failure after failure. Was God mocking him or was there some other way to be righteous before God? This gave the psalmist no end to his frustrations and caused his foot to almost slip. He was a regular at the house of worship and he gave his tithes and offering on a regular basis. The ministers had promised him that if he gave that it would return to him ten-fold pressed down, shaken together and running over. But from his experience none of this had come true in his life. However, this he did notice, and that was when he had given up trying to live the righteous life, it appeared that he experienced success. Could it be that the righteous life has already been lived for him?

Whenever his foot would stumble there was no lack of condemnation from his friends and neighbors, it was as if they were waiting for him to fall so that they could condemn him. He was never at a loss for accusers and for finger pointers. They were in abundance, even though they themselves were experiencing the same failures in trying to live the righteous life they delighted in throwing stones in his directions. Is this the design that God has for us? Have we been placed here to just hold-on until we see God and hope that he is merciful to us? The cycle of shame and guilt was too

---

[5] Romans 8:3

much for the psalmist so he poured his heart out to the only one who can do anything about it. He prays,

"Lord, surely you have provided a better way for me to live and be pleasing in your sight."

His mind faded back to the time when he was looking for his lost sheep and he fell into a deep pit that had been set to capture wild animals. There was no way out of the deep pit and there was no one to hear his screams and cries though they went on for hours and hours. It was here that his belief in God was about to be changed forever. In the middle of his cries for help he began to speculate as to why God had allowed him to fall into this deep pit. Was it because of the sins that he had committed and now God was angry with him and punishing him? Was it because he had not confessed to his sins quick enough to be pleasing with God? Was it because he had not brought all of his tithes and offerings to the storehouse and had kept some of them for himself? Or was it because he had failed to make the proper sacrifice for the sins of the flesh? Whatever it was it appeared that God was angry with him and had allowed this trial to come and test him. All of these questions began going through his mind as he contemplated his soon coming death.

God's pits have a way of changing your beliefs towards him. It was here that he received his finest revelation on how the righteous life should be lived. When he had finally given up hope and had come to the conclusion that his sins were the reasons for his tragedy, he saw a different side of God than that to which he was accustomed. It did not come from a minister nor from religion – it came from his personal experience with God. God sent someone to his pit in order that his life could be spared.

He had made no sacrifices to God for his sins and yet God had spared him. He had made no confessions of and yet God had extended his grace to him. No bargains were struck, no pleas were made. God had waited until he had absolutely nothing to offer him before he showed him his grace and mercy. The psalmist had been resigned to die in that pit of miry clay until God decided that he should live not because of who and what the psalmist was but because of who and what God is.

His personal experience with God was totally opposite of what he was used to hearing. God was an awesome God to be feared and exacting just punishment for a person's sin, and he records of sin and he waited until the right moment to bring down condemnation and judgment. He was not this forgiving and loving God that spared men.

So, when the psalmist was finally pulled from his pit his relationship to God was changed dramatically. It was no longer based on fear and loathing and having to look over your shoulder in fear and in doubt about where you stood before God.

"Lord, you don't want sacrifices on your alter or I would give them to you. You want a broken and contrite heart."

God no longer carried a big stick and a frown on his face, so the psalmist actually looked forward to being with God on a daily basis. In his heart he sang new songs of joy and deliverance. He spoke of how blessed is the man who transgressions have been forgiven and has his sins covered. How wonderful a God that does not condemn us with guilt and shame.

The psalmist praised God because in his new relationship to God he knew that he wanted to guide him with his eyes upon him daily and to give him instructions through his Holy Spirit. The mule and the horse need bit and bridle but God does not want to place a bit and bridle in the mouth and on the tongue of his people.

When God spoke to the psalmist he declared him to be righteous before him. He reminded him that there will be a new law. Not one like the ones that Moses handed down on Sinai, but one that has been written on his heart. The heart of stone would be taken from him and a new heart would be given to him. It was a heart that made room for God.

The psalmist had been given some new shoes for walking with God, a new robe to cover his nakedness before God, and a new ring that gave him authority and identity. The new shoes that God had given to him were not like the old shoes that were man made and wore out after a few months; these new shoes would never wear out and would help him to walk for the rest of his life. The old shoes represented his walk with Moses that led him down paths that were never ending and the footing was difficult and treacherous. Many have walked these paths with the shoes of Moses and their carnage was evident. The new shoes represented a different relationship that he now had as he walked with God. It was a relationship that brought him peace with God and with man. God was no longer displeased with him and held him to a standard that he could not keep. The old shoes of Moses brought disharmony and disunity among people and nations but the new shoes were able to walk pass the walls and around the barriers of division among men.

The new robe that the psalmist was given by the Father represented a life of righteousness and righteous living. The old life under Moses led him to a life of sin and regret and a never ending effort to please God. The fiery darts of the men were constantly aimed at the heart that was wounded and bleeding. But the life of righteous that God gave him was able to quench all of the maliciousness and slander of men. This robe was the same one that God gave to Adam and Eve to replace their fig leaves. Their efforts to cover their shame and guilt were not adequate before God. So he gave them his righteousness which covered their nakedness. It was the same robe that he gave to Abraham after he had committed adultery with Hagar; to cover his nakedness before God; it was the same robe that he gave to Jacob after he stole the birthright of Esau, it was the same robe that he gave to Moses after he killed the Egyptian and hid him in the sand, it was the same robe that he gave the king of Israel after he had committed adultery with Bathsheba, and now he has given the robe of righteousness to the psalmist that covered his sin. The lessons from the pits were numerous and life changing especially the lesson on the righteousness of God because all who stand before God must stand before him open and naked; there is nothing that is hidden from the eyes of God with whom we all have to do. But the psalmist knew that when he stood before God that he would not see eyes of judgment or eyes of condemnation but eyes of love and acceptance from God. It will be the eyes that Adam and Eve saw when God came looking for them, it will be the eyes that Cain saw that could have killed him after he killed his brother, but there was no look of judgment.

So, the psalmist is now free to love someone who first loved him. He delights to do the will of God now that there is no big stick hanging over his head. He knows that God is pleased with him and his service to him. But the one who stands before God in a defiant posture will have his heart exposed before him and the secrets that have been hidden from all but his Creator will be made known. God has not given him a robe of righteousness to cover himself; so as a result his conscious will not have a hiding place or find comfort before a holy God. It is not so much as God desiring to judge him as he has judged himself and tied the hands of God by refusing the robe of righteousness.

Many have refused to wear the robe provided by God and so, when they stand before him he is resigned to say, "Thy will be done" or they will say to God, "Thy will has been done." The naked soul is laid bare and nothing is hidden from the heat therein just as the sun rises in the east and sets in the west and nothing is hidden from its heat. But for the psalmist, this robe was not only a covering for him but it was also an invitation to a wedding feast that was given by God the Father. Without this robe, he would not be able to enter the kingdom of God.

Last of all the psalmist has been given a ring for his finger which signifies his place before God and his identity with God. The ring meant that you belonged to the Father, and that you are identified by the Father and have been given authority by the same. The psalmist knew that before the men of his day, his name had been slandered and that their tongues were like sharp knives that slashed away at his life and soul. But this was not true of God the Father. God never slandered him before men and never condemned him. God the fathers love was unconditional towards the psalmist and his mercies were new every morning. Men were quick to point out his shortcomings but God long on mercy and grace and knew that he was but dust.

Men were quick to remove him from his place in society but that was not true with God because his gifts and callings are without repentance. God does not throw men out with the trash as man do here on earth, for he realizes that a life is not defined by a few events and failure in a person's life. God the Father in his new relationship with the psalmist put a ring on his finger and restored him to his place and position before him.

The psalmist delighted to do the will of God.

Chapter Four

JOSHUA, SIN, AND RIGHTEOUSNESS

Down the hill and up the dirt road about 2 to 3 miles from my little shack in Mulberry, you will run onto an old asphalt road with the tar oozing out on top and road kills scattered along the highway. On the long hot dog days of summer, I would walk down to my friend Ronnie and sit and visit for a spell. Ronnie was tall thin, light-skinned and the unelected leader of our little gang in Mulberry. A bunch of us rag-tag younguns' would often meet at his house for a rousing game of baseball. We didn't always have a proper bat and ball so we played with just about anything that we could get a rag around or could kick. Ronnie absolutely loved to play baseball and when he wasn't plowing the fields or we weren't hauling hay for his father, the game was on.

"Put it right here," he'd always say.

"Put it right across the plate so I can get a piece of it."

His rear end would stick out towards the west and his chest towards the east. It was quite a sight; he would wobble the stick in his hand round and round. And sure enough when I put it right across the plate he would knock the socks off whatever it was wrapped around. Then he would let out this loud ahhhh ... as if he had done something really special and was extremely proud of himself. He would then proceed to do the Ichabod Crane strut around each base while my poor brother was still chasing the ball into the next county. After my brother finally hounded the ball down in the cornfield across the road, Ronnie was already at home plate and sipping on his lemon ice tea that his mother made for us. Whenever we got too close to his ice tea, he would have a tendency to place it well out of reach.

Ronnie was also our resident philosopher, he seemingly had an answer for just about everything and for everybody who ventured to ask, and it was no different when it came to the issue of God. I was always completely in the dark when the conversation turned to religious things and questions about God. I knew there had to be something out there; I just didn't know what it was or who it was. One thing that was completely evident in Mulberry was God's creation. It was and still is a constant witness of God's sovereignty. So, I knew that there had to be a God somewhere, I just couldn't put the puzzle together. Ronnie and I would lie on our backs and would look up at the sky and to the horizon and wonder about that Supreme Being. We always had a big ole' wad of sour dot weed in our mouths that we had plucked up from the ground and would chew on during our conversation. Sour dots are just about the most bitter weed that you can chew on and I really don't know why we ate it with the exception that the old folks told us that it was good for us. I have asked myself several times what it was good for because for the life of me I can't think of one thing that it has helped cure. I think we liked it because it was a lot like pickles; and we absolutely loved crunching into a big ole'sour pickle that had been soaked in vinegar. Sour dot had the same effect on people.

Well right there in the middle of the pasture we would look up at those pale blue skies over Mulberry and inevitably our conversation would turn to God. The combination of the witness of creation without and the witness of our conscious within was too great for us to ignore. We knew there was a God. This kind of creation didn't just happen to come about. Ronnie would alarm everyone silly with all of his dumb questions and accusations about God ranging from "I wonder what he is like" to "I wonder what hell is like if one day we get thrown into hell like a sack of old rotten potatoes." We scared each other out of our wits but not enough for us to stop chasing eligible young ladies. The right Reverend didn't help on Sunday morning with his hell fire and brimstone preaching, so I always figured, from his preaching that I had one foot in hell and the other on a banana peel and something needed to be done quickly.

A HUDDLE FOR RIGHTEOUSNESS

Thus, I started out on my journey in search for God but after listening to the resident philosopher Ronnie I didn't want to be scared out of my wits again; I figured maybe I should give somebody else a try.

One day as my bare feet were strolling against the part wood and part broken linoleum floor I came across what I thought might be some answers. About five of my aunts were carrying on this conversation about how bad men are; I figured maybe I can gleam some information from some of them in order not to be as bad as the rest of the men. I quickly got me an old wooden chair with the straw bands stretching from side to side and a hole in the middle. We, as a family were awfully fond of holes, we have a hole in the north wall, a hole in our straw band chairs, and a hole in the bottom of our shoes, and the last time I went to the doctor there was a hole in my underwear. We loved holes. So, I decided that I would have me some set-down right in the midst of this entire boyfriend bashing.

Now just as I was dragging my chair up between my two aunts, Ruby and Lucy, Aunt Ruby gives me this, "What on earth would cause you to do this scowl?" She barked at me.

"Puppies don't belong in bulldogs' conversation, now get out."

I was hurt because the conversation was really interesting. I didn't know men were as bad as all that they talked about. According to them all men must have just climbed out of some primeval pool and needed to be hit on the head every chance you got. I was getting a bit concerned for my safety when one of my more civil aunts stepped in and saved my life. I was already on a banana peel on my way to hell and Ruby was just about ready to finish the job.

Later, we had some set-down and had a long conversation about God and even about hell. My aunt Ruby figured out that if I was on my way to hell that it was her job to scare me back into heaven.

"Hell," she said, "yeah, let me tell you about hell. Boy, if you don't get right with God you are going to be a wiener roast in hell forever, and that fire in hell is really hot. It will singe your eyebrows at 40 paces. So you'd better get right with God or one day he will send you to this awful place for as long as you live."

That did it! I was getting saved for sure. Between Ruby, Ronnie, and Rev. Blanton, I was a basket case. Ruby had me in hell even before God did. She would have made an excellent evangelist in somebody's church. Secretly I think that she was still mad at me for breaking in on their all-girls and no-boys-allowed conversation and she had the needle out just a bit.

Nevertheless, I had to figure out how to get saved and to avoid this evil awful place that my aunt was yelling about. According to her I must have been the scum of the earth and I deserved to go to that awful place unless I repented and got right with God, which I had only already done 7369 times in the last year in church alone. I was getting a pretty good impression from Ruby and Ronnie that this God that they were talking about was primarily a person to be avoided and that he had this big sword that was drawn back with his right arm and that he was watching me with the thought of just waiting for the 7370th sin and that sword was going to come whistling down on me. So in my earlier years God was someone who was displeased with me until he got his extortion money and my attendance in church from 9:00 a.m. to 2:30 p.m.

The question was; how do I get right with God and get in his good graces?

Early one Sunday morning a bunch of us country cousins were fidgeting around on the back church pews, we certainly didn't want to go anywhere near the front because we might actually have to listen to the preacher and that was the kiss of death for a 10 year old. All of a sudden we heard this loud hoop and scream. I looked up and tried my best to find out which direction it was coming from. If the preacher wanted us young folks to listen this sure did the trick. Once I located from whence the scream came, I realized that the preacher's wife was playing on the piano one moment and the next thing I knew she was doing cartwheels, screaming to the top of her lungs and pulling and yanking on Cuttin Len's body. I remember thinking what in the world has gotten into this woman. Did she forget to take her medicine or is she demon possessed?

This went on surrounding Cuttin Len for a minute or two but to me it seemed like an eternity. If I wanted a better show I couldn't have paid to see one at the nickel and dime theater than this one. Then Sister Blanton began pulling on his arms and yelling out to him something that I have never understood to this day. I don't know what it was but it finally worked on Cuttin Len. His wife who was sitting next to him was paralyzed and in shock along with everybody else in the church. If you would have taken a picture of us five boys on the back row of the Union Road Baptist Church you would have seen ten pairs of hands clutching on to the back part of the pews and five sets of eyes peering just over the top of the pews. We were petrified, but we still couldn't figure out why we were petrified.

Finally, after five long minutes; it seemed like forever, of this and Sister Blanton about to run out of steam, the tears began to run down the old man's face. Cuttin Len very slowly and reluctantly got up from his seat and walked down the isle of the church and sat down in the sinner's seat. He took the preacher's hand and prayed. Finally, after Sister Blanton stopped the gyrations and went back to playing piano again, a long time sinner had at last gotten saved. They had been praying for Cuttin Len for a long time and now that he was old he had never joined the church and gotten saved. It was the most exciting day in church that I had ever been a part of and for a brief moment in time five boys on the back seat of the church stopped fidgeting, if for no other reason than we didn't want Sister Blanton coming after us.

Finally, when everyone went outside, one of the church members was missing. So we all went back inside and found Sister Gentry passed out beneath the pew, apparently the service had been a little too much for her.

Later on that afternoon my grandfather gave his take on what happened in the service. And told us that if Cuttin Len hadn't gone forward and joined the church after what Sister Blanton did he would have surely gone to hell. I remember thinking, "That's it. That is how you get saved and find God." So I plotted and planned once again my day of salvation, but there was only one thing missing; advice from the resident philosopher Ronnie.

Ronnie would give me the low down about getting saved and what to do. I could always depend on him to steer me towards the right direction. Later, we had ourselves some set-down and talked about joining the church.

"So, Ronnie, what do I do to get saved and to keep from going to hell?"

"Well, when the preacher opens the doors of the church that's when you go forward and tell him you want to get saved and not go to hell."

I went home after that enlightening counsel and thought it over for a day or two and prayed about it. This coming Sunday, I would summon up enough courage to do it. What was a week seemed like two years and then a lifetime, but Sunday finally came. I put on my Sunday best and that included as much bravado as I could muster. Then 9:45 and Sunday school came round and my heart was pounding harder than John Henry's hammer. The 11:00 service finally rolled around and I was about to have a heart attack at ten years of age. I can see the headlines now as they read, "Ten year old gets saved; then has a heart attack and dies, and goes straight to heaven." I don't know how many times I talked myself out of going forward to get saved but it must have been twenty-eight times within the same hour. I think I made about forty-eight trips back and forth to the bathroom trying to keep my kidneys and stomach in order.

At 12:30 the preacher began winding down his sermon and Cousin Martha decided that she wasn't going to get happy and shout any more and be slain in the Spirit. The choir, all three and half of them, dragged through the invitation hymn like they had molasses running through their veins, until one of the deacons finally brought out the chair; 'the sinner's chair'. Whenever this happened and you sat down in the sinner's seat, it was like someone had branded you with an A on your forehead for the rest of your life. Sitting in the sinner's chair meant that you were admitting what everybody else already knew (which they would not tell you to your face) and that being that you were the scum of the earth, and on this day you were repenting of your scum of the earth duties so that Jesus could save you.

After Bubba Charlie brought out the sinner's seat, I could have sworn that it looked much the same as old Sparky that the people used to talk about in Angola State Penitentiary. I didn't know if I was going to be electrocuted or get saved.

My legs weighed a thousand pounds a piece as I went down the aisle and confessed to being a dirty, rotten ten year sinner who rolled Mr. Willie's car down the hill on Halloween night. The Lord had finally caught up to me for my sins. The preacher rejoiced, my family was happy, and the church was ready to hear another round of "O Sinner has come home" by the choir, all three and half of them.

Rev. Blanton shook my hand and gave me the right hand of fellowship and I finally let out all the air that I had been holding in for a week. I was finally saved. The smile started on one end of my cheek and spread to the other. It didn't come off me for fourteen days. I was so happy that I wasn't going to that awful place where my Aunt Ruby had condemned me to just a few weeks ago.

Two weeks later I was sleeping very peacefully and in my dream and I heard this loud bodacious knock on my door. It was the kind of knock that a person does who knows you. "Let me reintroduce myself, I am the scum of the earth that you had left at the altar at the Union Road Baptist Church." It had up and followed me back home like some lost cat that keeps finding its way home. I shouted to the top of my voice,

"Get out! I left you for good back at the church altar. Why have you returned here?"

I tried to slam the door in its face but it would have none of it. Its right foot was logged just to the inside of the door so that I couldn't shut him out. Our conversation moved from a shouting match to a civil conversation and then to quiet tones of acceptance. Panic ran across my mind as I knew that I had gotten saved at the church so why were my sins returning to me even after I repented? I so much wanted to enjoy my new found freedom in Jesus Christ and in his church but here was this old intruder returning to spoil our fellowship. It didn't ask for permission to return home, it just barged through the door with its entire luggage like it had never left home before. So, what was I to do, how do this square with me and my new found relationship?

Four years after I had joined the church, the pastor decided that it might be a good time to baptize those of us who had joined the church – all three of us. People were not exactly beating the doors down to get into Union Road Baptist Church. And one Sunday after service we got dressed in some old clothes covered by our white sheets, and drove to the pond down from Cuttin Lens' house. We stopped right beneath a grove of large 40 foot oak trees that guarded the premises. Just to the other side of the barbwire fence was the pond that the cows drank from, the horses bathed in, and anything else that passed in that direction used this pond for everything except a baptismal pond.

The pastor brought with him this long pole with which he would measure the depth of the pool into which we were to get baptized. All of this was looking very shaky to me but I thought to myself that joining the church didn't get rid of the scum of the earth maybe being baptized will do the trick, so I was ready for baptism.

When we crossed over and through the rusted old barbwire fence we began to get some of the longest and strangest looks from the locals, not the two legged kind, but the four legged kind, who were wondering what the fuss was all about, and why we were in their pasture.

The preacher began placing his pole in the water to find us a place to walk in and be baptized. The water was nice and blue when we started but as soon as we took our first step it changed to a sandy brown from the muck on the bottom of it. My feet became so well stuck to the mud-and-clay mixture at the bottom of the pool that you could hear this giant sucking sound when I lifted my feet out of the miry clay.

Now the water moccasins that had slithered to the banks to check this all out were not exactly excited to see us coming to their pond and muddying up the place. I have never heard so much hissing and seen so much spitting in all my life. They were fairly put out to say the least.

Finally, we waded out about waist high in this pond amid all the snapping turtles that had finished drying off and had submerged themselves once again. Then the pastor prays for me grabs me by

A HUDDLE FOR RIGHTEOUSNESS

the nose (and I'm thinking please make this quick) and plunges me under the murky brown water. He looks at the crowds standing on the banks and says, "Buried in baptism and raised to walk in newness of life," and just like that it was over. We sang a few hymns out of tune, of course, but with all the vigor we could muster. The moccasins and turtles were glad to see us go; it was good riddance as far as they were concerned. However, on our way back to the dirt top road we picked up a few visitors along the way, and spent the night pulling them from under our armpits and legs once they had gorged themselves on our blood.

Rev. Blanton was happy and excited! However, the way that we had gotten to know him was not the best way for a preacher to introduce himself. My mother had decided to join his church right after he had given us a visit and consumed all of the chicken on the dinner plates. And even then he had a suspicious look on my chicken to which I held on tight.

We first started out with him in a little holiness church about two miles due south of us and the end of the dirt road. It was a small white church with a steeple in the middle and a hole in the floor. The hole in the floor was so that the snakes and lizards could join in on the worship service. As I said, people weren't exactly beating the door down to get in to our little church at the end of the road. Now Sister Blanton was playing her favorite tune on the snaggletooth piano. One of her favorites was *"What Cha gon' to do when the worlds on fire."* She loved to sing that song and watch the congregation (all five of us) go into panic attacks. My mother would get happy. It's an old fashion term for people who were touched by the Spirit, supposedly. It began with a loud war hoop most similar to what Sitting Bull would do right before he attacked Custer. Next, the body went into all sorts of gyrations and stretching routines. And if they were really smitten they would roll around on the floor for a few minutes between the pews until they passed out.

That is what I suffered through for over 20 years in my life, and the preacher would not conclude his sermon until some sister shouted and got happy. I always knew that was a bit on the suspect level much like the con man who talks to his victims until he had swindled them out of money.

Therefore, with the combination of Rev. Blanton's preaching and Sister Blanton's song, I was once again scared out of my wits. I knew what I was going to do if the world caught on fire. I was going to run and hide. If Jesus wanted me he was going to find me in the bottom of the cellar that we had built with the rest of the preserves. After leaving Rev. Blanton's service I didn't know whether I should spit or whistle, but I did know that I would be in the cellar if there was any inkling of a fire.

Rev. and Sister Blanton loved to come for Sunday visits, right after my mother had finished cooking the chicken. And, I somehow noticed that there was a correlation between the two. Now he would also leave when the chicken plate was empty. Daddy never did like the right reverend for some reason or other. The best we could figure out was that our chicken coop was seeing less and less chickens and when he left we had a surplus again. Go figure! Now my Aunt Ruby and her sister Georgia were enticed to sing at the little white church at the end of the road. Whenever people are asked to sing songs or solos in church it is considered an honor to do so and the recipient and the congregation are supposed to be blessed by it. On quite a few occasions not too many of us got blessed. The spirit was willing but the voice had gone south for the winter, yet on this blessed occasion Ruby and Georgia held their own much to my surprise. I had been the victim of their attempts at singing at home and let me tell you I wasn't willing to go through any of that again. At times it would get to the point to where Daddy would say, "Ruuubbyy, Georgia, please," and they would finally get the message. Bless their little hearts, but on this blessed Sunday Rev. Blanton seemed to be pleased. I guess he would have accepted anything to stop Sister Blanton's tirade about the world being on fire, and where ya gonna hide. Rev. Blanton was tapping his feet to the beat so I guess at least he was getting the blessings. It was hard for me to figure him out. Was he an angel of light or an angel of darkness?

Chapter Five

In 520 B.C. there was another preacher who had fallen through the cracks. He had returned with the exiles from captivity; a long 70 year captivity for the nation of Israel. Daniel, the prophet, had encouraged him and had told him that the time of captivity was over and done and that it was time for the Jews to return to the nation of Israel. The heavens above Babylon were buzzing with activity. Supernatural activities! For just a few days ago, one of the evil angels had intercepted a messenger that had crossed into his territory with plans for the future of Israel. They were good plans, plans for Israel to prosper and be at peace but this was not to the liking of the evil angel. For as long as there is war, strife, and the absence of peace, the evil angels are happy. If peace was allowed to prevail then perhaps God had a chance to communicate and fellowship with his people and that would not be good news for the evil one and his kingdom of darkness.

Finally, after 21 days of captivity, Michael, one of the chief princes in God's cabinet, was released and brought a fairly big stick with him to set the messenger with the future plans for Israel free. Once the dark angel saw Michael coming towards him in the power and authority of the Lord it was all over but the shouting.

"Release your prisoner at once for he has a message that must be delivered to God's people at once."

There was a slight hesitancy but no argument. Michael was the guardian of God's people and an angel much like him had destroyed the entire Assyrian army of 185,000 men in one night.[6] The good angel was immediately released to give the message to Daniel.

Daniel passed the good news on to his people. He was excited and enthusiastic that Israel was now free and could begin the

---

[6] 2Kings 19:35

process of returning to their homeland. The news was met with skepticism and lethargy, because of the many that had originally gone into captivity had long since died, and the younger generation had assimilated themselves into Persian culture and society and had become prosperous.

Thus, Daniel had his work cut out for him and so did Joshua, the high priest who was leading 50,000 captives back into the land of Canaan. When they arrived in late 538 B.C., the place was in shambles. There was no temple in the city of Jerusalem, the people who had been left had married into the surrounding nations and the Jews had no identity as a nation and as a people of God. Pagan worship was the order of the day as there were idols in every area of the old city.

Where the temple once stood were old cracked and bleached-out boulders that once held the temple of God in place. Tall grass covered many of the broken and scattered pieces of rock where the edifice once stood. Joshua fell down on his face and wept bitterly. The young people around him did not understand what all the commotion was about. Why the weeping and wailing. What was it that had Joshua so upset? Zechariah, the prophet, picked him up off his face and pointed him toward heaven as the two old men prayed to God for restoration.

After two years of hard labor and backbreaking work, the foundation for the temple had been laid. The young people who had prospered as captors were very reluctant to help in the rebuilding of the temple. They wanted to get on with their lives and to prosper as they did back in Babylon. For the life of them they couldn't figure out why these old men were making such a fuss over the rebuilding of the temple. Their attitude was; "we were just fine without God in Babylon – so why do we need him now?"

Thus, not everyone was pleased with the rebuilding of the temple. The neighbors were beginning to be concerned because they could see their profits going out of the window. The neighborhood committees on zoning met to discuss the rebuilding of the temple without their permission and they sent in Sanballot as their representative. Sanballot weighed around 300 pounds on any given day and that is being very generous. He had a long chewed off hay stalk stuck to the side of his mouth, and he rode a small donkey that had its tongue sticking out the majority of the time. Sanballot loved to sing, if you want to call it that, and everyone knew when he was in the neighborhood because you could hear him long before you saw him.

So, on that day, he pulled his tired old donkey up to the temple site where all of the rebuilding was taking place, and he reluctantly got off his mount. He first offered his help but he was soundly refused by Joshua and Zechariah. He felt miffed! Then he pulled out his long list of do's and don'ts handed out by the zoning committee to Joshua the high priest.

"Joshua, the committee forbids you to rebuild on this property and sent me to tell you to stop at once."

Joshua quickly became upset with Sanballot because he had told him repeatedly that his company and his advice were not needed.

"Sanballot – let it be known to you and your committee that this is the work of God, done by the people of God, and we will continue to rebuild the temple."

Sanballot left in a huff, belching out his favorite song to the top of his lungs much to the dismay of his neighbors. He is thinking and feels in his heart that there was more than one way to skin this cat.

So, later that night, he and several others came back into the city in order to destroy the temple. The rocks and cornerstones were laid to waste, the foundation of the temple that had taken them two years to build was destroyed, and the hearts of the people who had worked so long and hard to rebuild the temple were destroyed.

Later on that same night Sanballot returned to do further damage but Joshua, the high priest, caught him. An argument broke out. It escalated into a shouting match as Joshua the high priest in the darkness did something that no priest or preacher should have done.

Sanballot left and waddled back into his home and neighborhood. The damage had been done this night, and it was more than just the physical damage done to the site, there was spiritual damage done before God. Joshua returned to his home and he was depressed and mournful. He considered giving up the priesthood because of his sin against Sanballot.

His robes were not only dirty from his incident with Sanballot they were now dirty from his sins against God. The evil one had been there that night and knew what had happened and he now knew that he had grounds to bring a lawsuit against Joshua the high priest. This could be enough to sabotage God's future plans for Israel. The lawsuit would center on the right of Joshua to be the representative of Israel before a holy God seeing that Joshua was covered with sin. How could a righteous and holy God use an unrighteous and unholy man to accomplish his goals and plans for Israel? Priest and preacher are supposed to be perfect and holy and held to a higher standard. Joshua was neither! His *conduct did not match his confession* and so he should be disqualified from the priesthood.

Joshua had failed! His guilt was now a sledgehammer that the enemy could use against him on a daily basis and he was about to receive a summons for his misconduct.

Occasionally, God loves to hold meetings with all of his angels to catch up on the news and events around the world even as the angels view them. During these briefings, Satan is permitted to make his appearance and to present his case before God. On this particular day in the northern skies, angels showed up from every corner of the earth and from every nation on the face of the earth to give an account of what is happening in their area. The last one to be heard was Satan. He was bringing a lawsuit against Joshua the High Priest. The evil one had stood before God the Father many, many times in his life, he knew the court procedures, the protocol of God's courts, and he knew what the Judge himself was truly like. In the presentation of his case, there could be no cracks; his evidence against Joshua had to be solid and credible in order for it to stand up in court. So, in his entrapment of Joshua, his cause was airtight or else the Judge would throw out his case as he had done on so many other occasions.

Joshua had sinned against heaven and he was guilty; there was no doubt of that, but the enemy of Israel and God's people wanted Joshua judged and his title as high priest taken from him. He wanted

A HUDDLE FOR RIGHTEOUSNESS

the future of God's priestly nation in limbo for another thousand years and ultimately destroyed so that the plans of God would never come to fruition. Oh! The madness of such a quest, but this attorney did not lack great shrewdness and planning. He knew that God was faithful to Abraham and that he had kept his promises to Abraham. If he was faithful to Abraham then he would be faithful to Abraham's descendants. This meant that his evil empire would not stand, and this meant that in his scheming and planning he would need to attack the source of God's plan which was his priestly nation.

It was the same scheme that had been used with Cain and Abel. The source of God's righteous plan must be eliminated, and God had chosen to use the people of Israel to be the light of the world, thus the present darkness, hence the lawsuit against Joshua the High Priest. In actuality it was a backdoor accusation against the Judge himself. The enemy knew that God was a holy and righteous judge and that the judgments are true and righteous all together![7] This gave him an evil boldness to proceed with his lawsuit. When Joshua sinned against God and heaven, he had been baited and trapped into his sin. His old sinful nature had been taken advantage of and, of course, he needed to be judged.

The evil genius lurks in the darkness invisible to man. It is under the cover that he should be most effective. When Joshua sinned he blamed himself for his sin, he could not see and hear the invisible enemy around him planting thoughts and suggesting ideas into his mind and heart. When the enemy combines his suggestions with the impetus of an old sinful nature it is a lethal dose against any human being. Nevertheless, this is the job of the adversary in this case. His greatest weapon is deception and getting men to blame themselves for their sin rather than going to the real source of their sin. It has worked against Joshua and a host of others.

When the enemy stood before God the other lesser angel gawked at him and his beauty. He was extremely handsome in his appearance and stature. His garments were brilliant in their colors as his robe swept the floor. They wondered what could have caused such a

---

[7] Revelation 16:7

beautiful creation of God to go astray. His responses to the questions posed by the Judge were nothing less than well thought out strokes of genius. All types of precious jewels and stones glistened from his princely robe. He had an air of confidence that had descended into pride which was the cause of his downfall. He had a unique ability to sway millions of angels with his musical abilities. He was a magnificent creation and he now channeled all of his abilities to destroy God and his people.

One of the good angels asked himself the question; "Why does God allow evil and sin into his presence?" Sin has no effect on the power, presence, or on the position of God. The evil that Satan and his men and women have become is a perversion of the goodness of God. Evil is the flip side of good and of good intentions. It all happened when the evil one declared that he wanted to do things his way and under his own power. And having the awesome power of choice God allowed him to go his own way and to rebel. Satan took a third of the stars with him when he rebelled. He possessed so much power and influence that he influenced one third of God's elect angels to follow him to earth so that he could build his new kingdom to challenge the throne of God. Therefore God is unaffected because he does not have a nature that can be tempted to sin in any way shape or form.[8] Therefore, sin in the enemy or in man does not have any effect on God. Though he allows himself to grieve over sin yet he is not affected in such a way as to cause him to fall.

Consequently, it is man and Satan who are affected by sin and by the presence of God. Being in the very presence of God is a judgment against sin. This is the reason that God does not force anyone to be with him or to be in heaven because his very presence would be a torment to those who love darkness.

When the evil one stood before God he did not enjoy one moment of it. His evil brilliant mind wanted to do as much damage to Joshua before God as possible and then leave. He did not enjoy his accountability before God or the limitations that had been put

---

[8] James 1:13

on him. He loved rebellion though you would not know it from his appearance.

He thus began the presentation of his brief before God against Joshua the High Priest. The rap sheet on Joshua was long and extended. Every sin had been recorded in detail by the enemy as he appeared to delight in smearing God's people before the judge. The rap sheet on Joshua was indeed very long with a few blank sheets left at the end. If the high priest of the nation of Israel was sinful then, the nation of priests that were to be God's lights to a dark world; was sinful also. How can you represent a holy and righteous God by being a sinful priest? The implication was that Joshua needed to clean up his act before God before he could be called a representative of God. *His conduct did not match his confession* as a representative of God's Kingdom. Everyone knows that preachers and priests are supposed to be righteous, holy, and having no vices.

The good angels were watching intensely; looking on the proceedings with great interest and listening attentively to what was happening at this trial. The prosecutor had no love for the nations of Israel nor did he lack any evil intention towards them.

The brief had caused a scandal against Joshua the High Priest because not even the good angels could answer the brief that had been provided by Satan before the courts, for they, themselves, were not privy to the workings of God's redemptive plans seeing that they have never been redeemed themselves.

Joshua's status in Jerusalem went down considerably after his exposure through the lawsuit. His reputation had been damaged to the point that the rebuilding project in Jerusalem would not resume. The temple of God would have to be delayed for another hundred years. In his moment of deepest despair, Joshua's defense attorney came to him and spoke to his heart through his ears and said, "Not by power nor by might but by the spirit of the living God will the temple in Jerusalem be rebuilt." Joshua was so encouraged by his new attorney that the court had assigned to him; with that one whisper his life had been changed forever and he had received new hope. God's calling on his life would not be thwarted, not by the enemy, not by slander or persecution, nor by his sin that the enemy had exposed in his court case. The calling of God on his life would be fulfilled by God himself. The temple in Jerusalem would be rebuilt by God and not through his schemes and plans. Satan's case had been brilliantly crafted against Joshua and it was also judicially sound. It would stand up in any court of law where the truth was upheld. The enemy knew that Joshua was guilty of his sin before God and that if God was just and righteous as he had said in his word,[9] then Joshua must be found not only guilty but he must also come under the judgment of God himself.

Joshua's accuser stood at his right hand in court, and whenever you stand at someone's right hand in the eastern courts, it does not mean that you are innocent until proven guilty; it means you are guilty – period. Joshua was guilty and there wasn't any denying that. The evidence against him was conclusive, and his enemy was thoroughly enjoying every moment of this. He had the goods on Joshua; he had the Judge in a judicial hammerlock, and a verdict that was certain. His scheme and well thought out judicial traps were working to perfection. He had gotten the Judge to drop the gavel on other men of faith[10] so that he knew that his case was sound against Joshua. His scheme was as brilliant as the Hope diamond in the bag of a cat burglar who knows that he has just stolen something which is priceless. His briefs were argued with the cunning of a serpent and the motives of a preacher with a bank account in Switzerland. Would God's own character and His own standards of righteousness and holiness be used against Him in a court of law?

Throughout the ages trials have been known to take surprising twists and turns and this one was no different. Joshua's defense attorney took the floor and stood at the right hand of Joshua knowing that his client was also very guilty of sin against God. He had very wisely anticipated the schemes of his old court adversary and prosecuting attorney. The prosecutor was a day late and a dollar short in this case against Joshua.

---

[9] Rev 16:7
[10] Job 1-2

The angel of Jehovah turned on his adversary and jumped on him like a chicken on a June bug. He looked at Satan in the eye and then asked him a penetrating question. He said, "What if the sins of Joshua and the people of God have been paid for in advance?"[11]

He turned to the Judge and said, "Your honor, what would be the verdict against Joshua if God gave men a righteous and holy nature that was not subject to the judgment of the court?[12] Would not the judgment of God be thrown out?[13] Would he not have the right to be a minister of God?"

Then the angel of Jehovah reached to plant the ultimate nail in Satan's coffin. He turned to the jury and said, "Ladies and gentlemen of the jury, wouldn't it be wonderful if God gave to man his own righteousness?"[14]

There was a slight applause in the gallery. The good angels of God who were listening intently to this case and following the arguments of the Angel of Jehovah knew that he had struck a decisive blow to the argument of their old adversary. Joshua's eyes looked into the face of the Judge and saw that there was no condemnation, that he could not be judged because of the provision that God had made for him. There was hope. There was great hope. The gallery was cheering and shouting much to the dismay of the judge who had threatened to empty his courtroom if the shouting did not stop. His warning and rapping of his gavel went unheeded for a few moments because of the sure joy of being free. One of the members of the gallery quickly ran outside and shouted to a waiting audience what the angel of Jehovah had done to the courts of heaven. He had taken away the condemnation; he had nullified the judge's ability to bring down judgment against Joshua because of his sin. The roar of the crowds on the outside could be heard on the inside and it was getting nearly impossible for the judge to restore order no matter how hard he rapped with his gavel. What the enemy did not know was that

---

[11] Rev. 13:8; KJV Ps 32:3;130:3
[12] New Covenant, 2 Pet. 1:4
[13] Rom. 8:1, Eph. 1:4
[14] Romans 5:19

God had already anticipated his own dilemma and his own conflict with the sin of man and his righteous and holy nature and that the sin of man had been provided for even from eternity past at the foundation of the world.[15] Order in the court finally came when the judge threatened for the final time to throw everyone out except the jury. There was a temporary calm because even though the gallery was quiet on the outside they were standing up and cheering on the inside. They knew that Joshua, even though he was a sinner, was about to be acquitted before God.

The Angel of Jehovah proceeded with his argument after order was restored and laid out a precedent that God had established with Abraham, when he and Isaac had finally reached the mountain of sacrifice in the land of Moriah. The Angel of Jehovah turned to the jury and repeated the questions that Isaac had asked of his father Abraham, "Father, where is the sacrifice to God?" Then the Angel of Jehovah in a very dramatic fashion approached the judge's bench and stared into his eyes, waited for silence and decorum to rejoin the court, and then said to the Judge,

"God will provide for himself a sacrifice."

Tears came into the heart of the Judge and into the eyes of the defense attorney. His argument was allowed by the court because God would provide a perfect sacrifice to meet his holy and righteous demands. God was the only one that could provide a sacrifice for himself and he was the only one that could appease himself. Joshua could stand before men and God now as a minister because of what God had done and not because his *conduct did not match his confession.*[16] The objections came hot and heavy from Joshua's accuser. He constantly reminded the Judge of his word which was binding and authoritative. But each objection was met with an overruling by the Judge. The defense attorney for Joshua had done his homework thoroughly and was quite prepared for the surprises of his adversary.

---

[15] Rev. 13:8, Eph. 1:4
[16] Rom. 6:11

A HUDDLE FOR RIGHTEOUSNESS

The courtroom scene that day was extremely tense because not only was a man's life on the line so was the future of Israel. The Judge looked at the defendant Joshua and told him to return in six months for his verdict and ruling.

The enemy recoiled and snarled at the decision of the court. He leered at the Judge with an angry and defiant look from the corner of his eye. He knew that he could go no further on this day with the case against Joshua. Evil, vicious and murderous eyes glared at the defendant as they left the courtroom. Joshua was shielded from the vicious stare of the evil one by the Angel of Jehovah. His anger quickly turned into rage, the same rage that was in Cain when he had killed Abel. The Judge quickly called for Michael to escort Joshua out of the courtroom and to his home.

Joshua knew very well that he had not heard the last from Satan; that his traps would be set again and again as his hatred for him and the nation of Israel knew no bounds.

Joshua was briefly escorted from the courtroom between the shoulders of Michael the guardian of Israel and the Angel of Jehovah to a safe place until things could cool down.

There were all sorts of excited chatters by the lesser angels outside of the courtroom for they had just witnessed a major part of God's redemptive plan for man. They knew now that God was no longer in conflict with his nature and that he was no longer in the condemnation business.[17] Their discussion centered on the sins of men and how they were being dealt with legally and judicially. Is it entirely possible that man can have the righteousness of God credited to his account and meet the holy and righteous standards set by God when they come face to face with him? Is it possible that the sins of all mankind have been paid for? Oh, what an incredibly genial plan of God who has made provisions for all of his creation. The Angel of Jehovah did a reversal from the hammerlock position that had been put on him and Joshua; it would be a precedent for all of mankind. Satan had crumbled before the courts of heaven like a deck of falling cards. His scheme had been ripped to shreds more so

---

[17] Rom. 8:1

than a pair of worn out pants. This ruling if left to stand by the courts of heaven would reduce him and his power to the prodding of lies buried deep in the sinful nature of man in order to get us to believe his rhetoric. His best slight of hand trick would be to get men to believe that his thoughts are their thoughts.

Joshua retired to his home with Michael guarding him for a time. Michael was an extremely powerful angel, a cherub with incredible powers at his disposal. He was the seal upon Joshua's door that allowed no one to enter or come near. Meanwhile, inside; Joshua was in deep thought and meditation for several days as to what had just taken place in the courtrooms of heaven. He was still concerned about the future ruling of the Judge on his case, as he pondered the tactics and arguments set forth by the Angel of Jehovah. Why were there tears in his eyes when he faced the Judge and said, "The Lord will provide for himself a sacrifice"?

Men of his day had become so corrupt before God that no sacrifice would suffice for their sins. Is it possible that when Adam fell that the damage was so severe and the rift so large, that in order for us to be reconciled to God, the price that had to be paid was the life of the Creator? Was it now possible that God's standards for reconciliation was so high that it is impossible for man to ever think about being reconciled to a holy and righteous God? If God himself is the only one who can meet his standards then why does he need the sacrifices of bulls and goats? Is it possible that if God does not provide for us the redemption necessary then there will be no redemption?

Joshua began to ponder his life and he remembered that time after time whenever he lifted a standard and tried to live by it he failed under its weight.

Even with the failure to live under laws or standards Joshua still wore his high priestly robes from the trial. He noticed that his robes were stained from top to bottom.[18] They were not just ordinary stains but filthy stains that represented the holy life that he had lived and the holy standards that he had kept. He receded

---

[18] Zech. 3:3

back into the darkness of his room and sat in the shadows with his head between his knees. He had done his best to serve God but yet instead he was filthy. The weight of this depression was so heavy that he fell into a deep slumber and it was here that the Spirit of the Living god had time to speak to his heart. His dreams faded back to the time when Moses had come down from Mt. Sinai with the commandments of God. They had been written by the fingers of God when He had found the people of God participating in orgies and adulteries before God on his mountain. If the people of God could have kept the commandments of God then they would have been blessed. They would be blessed in their comings and goings in all that they did, but for Moses and the Hebrew children it would not be so. Moses became so angry that he threw the commandments down and broke them himself. No sooner had they left the fingers of God had they been broken. There had to be a better way to keep God's commandments.

Joshua awakened from his dream and found that his room was filled with darkness. He looked at his robe and it is still filthy. Would he ever wear a robe that was clean and white? He sat on his floor and gazed at the wall for hours at a time wondering about his fate as a minister of God. He knew that he was not worthy of the title of minister but yet he had been chosen by God. This office of the priesthood had made a mockery of his conscience and his life. He knew that he was living a lie but it had to be hidden from the people of Israel, he could not let them know what he was really like. In court the enemy of his soul had exposed him before man and God and his life was in shambles. The angel of Jehovah did a most wonderful job in his defense but the words of his enemy were incredibly damaging to his soul. He could not ignore them because he knew that the words of condemnation from the evil one was true and righteous. If he could have gotten out of this masquerade he would have done so a long time ago but the calling of the Lord is without repentance.

In the synagogue on Saturday mornings Joshua would read the word of God to the people of Israel. He could not let the people know that it had become meaningless to him and that it was hollow in his soul. He continued in his shallow existence and his loneliness. There was no one to minister to the minister. He had to be strong for the congregation but if they only knew that he was just as weak in his faith as they were they would have booted him out of the synagogue long ago. The very law that he preached on Saturday mornings was making a sham out of his life. He could not keep it; he could only pretend that he was holy. Any time he had lifted a standard and tried to live by it, he would crawl beneath that standard. The very law that he loved dearly had become a source of spiritual death for him. It appeared as if the very thing that was to be a source of hope and life for the people of Israel was bringing death to him and his people. However, his inner man was telling him a different story and that was that the law of God was good, righteous, and holy, but the law that was in his members was powerless to keep the commandments of God.

When Joshua retired for the night he went into a deep sleep and he had a vision. In his vision he saw Father Abraham who was struggling to keep the commands of God. And when Abraham had tried to keep the commands of the Lord, it had caused him to commit adultery with Hagar the Egyptian servant. Abraham was powerless to keep the commands of God and to live righteously before him. In his vision he saw Moses who knew that the calling of God was on his life and was moved to do what God had called him to do, which was to lead the Hebrew children out of bondage. In his efforts to fulfill his calling before God he looked for an opportunity do what he had been called to do. God showed him in the vision the presumption of Moses that God would be a part of his plan when God had other plans for Moses to lead the Hebrews out of Egypt.

Moses seized the moment and killed an Egyptian soldier and hid him in the sand thinking that the Hebrews would follow in his leadership, he had not stopped to think and ask God if this was a part of something that he wanted to do, instead he plunged ahead and tried to keep the calling of God in his own strength. It caused him to be a murderer. The vision took Joshua before the holy of holies in the temple and there he was going about his priestly duties before the nation of Israel. There was a very long rope tied to his leg for he knew that if he ever made a mistake in the holy of holies that it would be his last mistake and they would have to pull his dead body out of the temple for no one was going in to get him. And there in the temple he saw a man who was performing his duties for him boldly before the throne of God. And when he had finished the man did something that no priest had ever done in the holy of holy. When he had finished his work, he sat down. Joshua was in awe because the man who sat down in the temple was not struck dead by the power of God. When Joshua saw this he rested and then he slept.

Chapter Six

Around the corner and up the hall from Mrs. McIntire's first grade classroom was the place where you would find me again struggling through my school work. It was the school house version of Sing-Sing prison complete with a four foot eleven inch warden.

Now the trauma that I had in the first grade was nothing compared to what I was about to face. When you walked into the third grade at my school, you would find a skinny little woman who was always dressed in red. That is all that I can remember about Mrs. Platt with the exception of two events that scared the living daylights out of me. Now why there was a Mrs. in front of her name I could not tell you for the life of me. Why would anyone, in their right mind, want to marry a Tasmanian devil? I don't remember the education of the third grade but I do remember the "enforcer lady" from the third grade. She only weighed about 90 pounds soaking wet but that was a lot less than the kind of mean that she packed away. The entire third grade class lived in fear of this woman who did not know the difference between educating nine and ten year olds and being a marine sergeant.

It began one day all too clearly with us preparing to do the Christmas play. The third grade of my era was different from what you see today, the teachers during my day taught more than just the basics, they also taught music, physical education, and whatever else the administration could imposed upon their educative skills. In our preparation for the Christmas play each child would receive an instrument to play during our presentation of this moving gala event to our parents.

I did not have much choice in the matter of instruments that I could play seeing that the supplies were limited. So, Mrs. Platt pulled out something from the closet that neither she nor I recognized. As far as I know you were supposed to hit it as certain times during the singing of the Christmas carols and it made a ringing noise. It resembled something that we put around ole Betsy's neck so that we could find her when she got lost in the woods of Mulberry. I had no idea of what was going on or what she wanted me to do with this instrument.

So, the kids started with the singing of Silent Night and of course, I missed my cue. I was fascinated with the cow bell. The first time that I missed it, I received a royal chewing out from Mrs. Platt because I had not chimed in with the rest of the group. I figured the singing was bad enough so why should I make it worse by clanging on something at the end of the song, besides it sounded downright horrible.

Now the second time I missed my cue on the cow bell that was all she wrote. There was a sharp pain right across my right hand that was given as a reminder to hit the bell on time. I was shell-shocked. If she thought that she had problems with me hitting the bell on cue before; she really had a worst case on her hands after that. Not only was I fascinated with the cow bell, I was also keeping a sharp eye on the long stick in her right hand. To this day, I cannot tell you whether or not I got it right. But I do remember the whack on the knuckles. Back in the stone-age, the teachers, if they didn't have a belt to whip you with they made you go out and pick your own switch from the tall grass in the back of the school house. Lord help you if you came back with a twig; that just made them a whole lot madder. The thing that Mrs. Platt had asked me to do I did not have the ability to do. We didn't play instruments on the farm, we plowed fields and rode horses and planted gardens.

Soon after my little musical debut, a young lady by the name of Polly got on the good side of Mrs. Platt if you know what I mean. Polly did not like homework but she did like sleeping in class. On this fateful day, Polly did not do her homework as usual. It was all that Mrs. Platt could do to contain herself. She flew into a rage, Polly ran across the room, Mrs. Platt in her red dress chased after her, and it was the greatest show on earth that I have ever been a part of. All of us kids got to watch the action up close. She went to the

A HUDDLE FOR RIGHTEOUSNESS

closet again and pulled out her belt and started on Polly. Well, Polly didn't exactly want to cooperate with Mrs. Platt, so she ups and runs around the room with this tiny little terror after her. We all stood in wrapped attention. Mrs. Platt went for the legs, the head, the body, you name it, and the belt was flying every direction that you could think of. You could not make out what was being said because you did not know whether you wanted to listen or watch the action.

In the midst of the whipping you heard; "I told you Polly never to come back to this class again without your homework."

Whenever the belt landed you would hear this, "Oh Mrs. Platt, please don't hit no more." There were several screams like that which could be heard all over the school yard. This went on for about ten minutes until something happened that sent the class into an uproar. Poor Polly was finally cornered and rather than being hit by the belt she started backing up and trying to catch the belt in her hands before it got to her body. She was fairly successful until she ran into the trash can in the corner of the room and fell backwards into the trash. Her rear end was stuck in the bottom of the trash can and only her arms, legs, and head were sticking out. The entire class (including me) spent the next three days picking ourselves up off the floor from laughing so hard at Polly and Mrs. Platt.

When it was over there was a long awkward silence in the room, we didn't know whether to spit or whistle because we were dumbstruck between fear and laughter thinking that Polly had it coming to her. We didn't know that there was a better way of being disciplined. We did not know that there was a better method of teaching as opposed to the methods of Mrs. Platt, the tiny terrorist of her day. We could not keep her standards of laws and regulations. My life as a believer was much the same as my earlier grades in school. Surely there must be a better way to learn of God and his teachings. Keeping laws, rules, and standards was not the way. There was always a consistent failure in my efforts to try and keep God's word and commandments. There are too many Mrs. Platt's out there. Is there a better way to please God?

Chapter Seven

**THE OLD MOSES
AND THE LAWS OF RIGHTEOUSNESS**

The journey had been long for this small child from the backwoods of nowhere, but he had finally reached his destination. Through no fault of his own his search for God was beginning to pay off. The desert and wilderness that had been a part of his existence from childhood was now behind him and he would finally meet God face to face. The excitement inside him could barely be contained as he prepared to climb up the side of this barren mountain. God wanted him in private seeing that the other Hebrew children had opted out a long time ago. There on the side of this block of granite he heard a voice that sounded like a powerful waterfall. Moses stopped in his tracks as God said to him that this was where they would meet. Then a powerful finger was seen engraving the two stone tablets. God wrote His ten commandments on them for the Hebrews to follow.

Meanwhile, about 3000 feet below the Mount Sinai trouble is brewing in the form of Moses' antagonist, Korah. He has the camp in an uproar with the absence of Moses. According to him they should all go back to Egypt where they can find plenty of food to eat. Korah had been feuding with Moses ever since they had left Egypt. Moses was a thorn in his side and he absolutely disliked him though he never let it show. Whenever he greeted Moses there was a smile on his face as he exchanged greeting but beneath the smile he was seething and looking for every opportunity to displace Moses.

The hot sands of the Midian desert had given him a bitter taste in his mouth for this whole promise land trip. Moses had promised them a land flowing with milk and honey but so far all they had seen was a land running with cobras and scorpions and he was ticked at Moses. Whenever he was angry there was always a nervous tick that he had right beneath his chin. His lips would slightly quiver which was a nervous display of what was happening in his inside. He wanted to take over, he wanted to be in charge of things, and he was planning and scheming and waiting for the right moment. With Moses away he would seize his chance. Aaron was much too weak to stand up to him so he began to take charge and to lead in a rebellion against Moses. Korah was the son of Izhar, who was the son of Kohath and the son of Levi who was ordained to be a priest by the Hebrew children; yet he was a priest with ambition. We do not know whether or not his ambitions were pure and admirable, but what we do know is that he did not like Moses in the position that he was as the head of the Hebrew nation. So he plotted and he schemed against Moses. At first it was done secretly and only with his family but then he began to be blatant about what he was doing as he realized that he would need a great deal of help seeing that Moses was very popular with many of the Hebrews and he appeared to have the backing of El Shaddai. It never occurred to Korah once that he may have been wrong in his thinking and in his actions. It never dawned on him that it was God who had put Moses in his position as the leader of the Hebrews, but he was about to find out the hard way.

On his way down the side of the steep and treacherous Sinai, Moses picks up his faithful disciple Joshua who had helped the 80-year-old patriarch up the side of the mountain. On their descent, their conversation was interrupted by the sounds of music, loud music, drums beating, and lascivious dancing that the Hebrew women had learned from the Egyptian women. The men proceeded to follow them in their lead as they appeared to be celebrating the absence of any restraint now that Moses was gone.

Now that the cat was gone the rats were doing a whole lot more than just playing. This party with the golden calf in the middle had it going on strong. The supporters of Moses went back to their tents and yanked their wide-eyed children with them. This was the first time that they had to cover the eyes of heir children since they had left Egypt, for in Egypt activities like this was a daily occurrence and the order of the day. But they knew that they were the people of

God and called to be the light of the world. However, at this awful time and place the light wasn't even flickering, as matter of fact, it was completely out. They went back to their tent and prayed that God would be merciful in his judgment against them, for surely as they saw this His wrath would be upon them in a heart beat.

Where were Moses and Joshua when you needed them the most? Aaron was there but he was cowering in his tent along with the rest of the chickens, and Korah when he looked upon the scene, his ambitions knew no end; he would bring reform back to the people of the Hebrew nation. He would do what Moses had failed to do ever since they had come out of Egypt. He had known all along that the Hebrews belonged back into the nation of Egypt where they had good food and plenty of water from the Nile River, because in this God-forsaken place no water was to be found. Korah never considered that the reason they were in a dry and barren land was by design of someone who was much greater than he was and that He was watching his every move and knew his every scheme. He was about to find out the hard way.

So, he called on his faithful sidekick, a man by the name of Dathan, with whom he had shared his plans and aspirations. Korah the rebellious priest to the Hebrews was a small balding man in a fragile frame that had a large ego. Though he was small in stature and had been given the position of priest; he had the heart of a spitting Cobra. The poison of asps continually dripped from his lips as he masqueraded in the robes of a priest. No one suspected what he was really like because they regarded him as a priest of almighty God and you did not question the priest.

Korah despised Moses. He did not like what Moses stood for or what he represented; to him Moses was a false prophet who had wrangled his way into the priesthood and he looked forward to getting him out of the way. And so you would find him continually griping and grumbling about the conditions of the camp and wanting to go back to Egypt. He wasted no opportunity to complain about Moses as he stood poised behind every tree ready to strike at the heels of his prey. He slithered into as many tents as would hold to his company and would listen to his complaints against Moses. Over a few months time he had gathered quite a throng of disgruntled men, women, and priests who were furious at being taken out of Egypt and out from under the whip and rods of the Egyptians. Korah's opposition to Moses began when the people started looking to Moses for leadership when they were planning to leave Egypt. And now Korah was looking for every opportunity to stab Moses in the back until he could get his credibility back as a priest of the Hebrews. He had taken advantage of his position as priest in the Egyptian bondage and had robbed the people, who were under the lash and whip, every day. This preacher was the storm that returned after the heavy rains. Many ministers in the tribe of Levi excelled at what they did as priests but not Korah. He used his position to his advantage and milked the people who were in bondage for all that they had. It was not so much what he did but it was how he did it, using the name of God to pull off his evil deeds with none to suspect him of his crimes.

Korah had no intentions or desire to be a real priest; he was a man with deep, deep, ambition and wanted to become as wealthy as possible. He wanted power, privilege, and position and was willing to move any mountain to get it, including Sinai. Thus, as he sat coiled in his tent ready and waiting for the opportune moment to strike at the heels of Moses, he began to elaborate a scheme. Of course no one would suspect what was really behind the chaos he intended to create but there would be a method to his madness. God did not figure into his plans or his schemes. That usually happens to the desperately ambitious person who is disgruntled and displaced. God does not figure into their plans. Oh, he gave lip service to God, but in the end he was a tool to be used by Korah for his own gain and to reach his own selfish goals. Korah was evil!

This strategy to disrupt the plans of Moses was his most ambitious and evil yet. His conscience had been seared long ago during his scandal with the Hebrew people. So there was no appealing to the heart of this evil priest. The flock in the congregation was none the wiser because they believed that the priesthood of Korah could be trusted; they wanted so much to believe and to trust in God to take care of them. Korah was keen to take advantage of people's faith and their willingness to be guided spiritually. The path he threaded led to destruction and misery and he was leading a group of people to their ruin along with him.

Korah's evil scheme was a mixture of deception camouflaged with further lies. This is the nature of serpents. Serpents do not like to be seen. They love to blend in with their surroundings as to appear unseen but their effect is devastating.

Korah had masked his plan inside a complaint that Moses and Aaron had set themselves over the congregation and above the rest of the priest and tribal leaders.[19] It did not matter whether the complaint was true or not, Korah was only interested in its after-effects. He had no idea that Moses had declined this job forty years ago at the burning bush but God told him that he had to go to Egypt and to lead his people out of bondage. So his assumption was that Moses had put himself in this position when it was God who had put Moses in his position. Could it be that Korah was unknowingly fighting against the God of Moses rather than Moses himself? The second fold to his scheme was to claim that Moses had lied to them in not keeping his promise of taking them to the land flowing with milk and honey but was going to leave them in the desert to die.[20] He was emboldened to say flat out to Moses, "We are not going with you anywhere, Moses." The Lion that was tracking Korah was moving into a crouching position and preparing to strike.

The third lie of Korah was that Moses had arrogated the priesthood to himself and to Aaron to the exclusion of the other priests.

"Moses do you think you are the only one chosen by God to be priest, we are all priests, we are all capable of carrying the sensors before God"

All the while Dathan, Korah's accomplice, is watching all of this with a very nervous stomach. He quickly retreats inside his tent knowing that Korah was more than likely walking around with a trap door beneath him and that sooner or later it was going to give way beneath him. Nevertheless, he keeps a brave face not knowing

---

[19] Numbers 16:3
[20] Numbers 16:4

the outcome of the coup against Moses. He is playing both ends against the middle because he plans to be on the safe side if this thing gets out of hand. He plans to be with Korah if the rebellion succeeds, or to be with Moses if the rebellion does not succeed. So, he waits inside his tent and peeks through the flaps to observe the developments even though he is an integral part of Korah's plan.

Joshua, who is Moses' understudy, is watching the scene shaking his head in disbelief. He is devastated at the corruption of the priesthood that he has witnessed. Did they not see the plagues of Egypt and how they had brought down the most powerful man on the face of the earth while bringing an entire nation to its knees? Did they not witness the parting of the Red Sea and the destruction of Pharaoh's entire army? Did they not have manna when they needed it and quail for meat when they asked for it? These were not the deeds of a man. These were the deeds of someone who is much stronger than any manly power. Moses was a mere mortal; he could not have caused the fire at night and the clouds by day. He could not have caused water to come out from the rock.

Joshua knew that God was reaching his limits with the Hebrews in the wilderness. They were acting like spoiled children of royalty instead of being the light of the world. The light had become darkness and people seemed to prefer darkness over light. The game of Korah was being played out in the sight of God. It was a cat and mouse game to see how much you could get away with and how far you could push the All Mighty.

Korah had turned the truth into a lie and had made a lie into the truth even though what he said and what he did had no merit. He knew the tenet saying that 'if people believed a lie long enough they would eventually accept it as truth' and this is what Korah counted on. A masterpiece of deception mixed in with a tablespoon of anger and a pinch of jealousy; and you have a person who is on a trail of destruction that will come quickly. Korah was a time bomb waiting to go off. He was an accident waiting to happen. He was a disease that had to be cut out of the body to save the malady.

And, he was going to take as many people with him as he could if he was not successful. This all began when he exchanged the truth

A HUDDLE FOR RIGHTEOUSNESS

about God for a lie. He was receiving in his person the due penalty of his error and that was a heart that grew darker as time grew longer and repentance was out of reach. The congregation who believed in Moses watched as he fought against a power that was much greater than him and a foe that he could not see. Very shortly, the lion of the tribe of Judah that had been tracking him ever since he had hatched his plan; would come out of his lair and drag him away and there would be none to come to his rescue. Korah's game was about to be over, he was going to be checkmated. It was only a matter of time before the King turned his thumb down. He was a cancer looking for a body and now he was a body looking for a grave. In the end, he would find both.

Of course, Moses would have to be eliminated somehow and somewhere and that would be the time and place of their choosing. Dathan was a ruthless and heartless man in a five-foot frame and he was looking to share the spoils of the coup against Moses. He had a host of about two hundred and fifty men at his disposal to which Korah needed access. Once they had gotten organized they wanted Moses to have an accident on one of the mountains in the area where the boulders scattered below.

Just as Korah was about to make his move and to bring order to the place, Moses appeared with a glare in his eyes and an extremely red face. The red face was not exactly from the 120 degree heat of the desert. He was not upset, he was not angry, Moses was absolutely livid with what he was witnessing among the light of the world, the priests to the nations of the world.

The Hebrews looked up and saw him standing on the side of the mountain with two tablets of stone in his arms which had been given to him and written by the hand of God himself. There was an awkward silence between Moses and the people. It was the kind of silence that went on for ten minutes. It was the kind of silence that your parents give you when you know you have a beating coming. Moses descended a bit closer to get a better look at things, to sort everything out, so that there would be no mistake as to who would be able to continue on his journey to Canaan land. Korah, Dathan, and now Abiram watched carefully as he descended. He saw embarrassed men and women putting their clothing back where they should have remained in the first place. The supporters of Moses stuck their heads out of the tent flaps as Moses was now walking among the Hebrews to assess the damage being done. The farther he walked, the redder his face became. The folks in the tents knew something hard was about to come down. Dathan whispered to Korah that this would be the perfect time to take Moses because they would never have another opportunity like this one. It never occurred to Dathan that someone was watching him and protecting the one they wanted to destroy. He would soon learn the hard way.

Moses' anger was such that it was controlling his body and mind. God had warned him previously and time after time about his anger but Moses had no way of subduing it. It was either going to come out against the Hebrews or Moses would have an ulcer from trying to contain the ire within him.

It was when he saw the golden calf that the gates of Hades broke loose. The very commandment's that were written by the hand of God and would bring a blessing to the people of God were in danger of being broken. He threw the tablets of stone directly against the golden calf and they shattered into a thousand pieces. In a fit of temper he took the calf and destroyed it, grinding it into pieces and made those responsible drink the lead from the calf. When Aaron saw this he ran away as fast as his ninety-year-old legs could take him. Moses caught him and pinned him down to ask him why he had done such a thing and sinned against God. The eyes of Moses were like small black beads that rage had twisted and shrank into something that Aaron did not recognize. Fearing for his life Aaron came up with anything but the truth when he said, "My Lord, when I threw the metal into the fire the calf jumped out." Moses was much too angry to find the humor in Aaron. He had the look of a man who was possessed but not by his God.

Now, not only was Moses angry, El Shaddai was most upset with the Hebrews to the point of wanting to destroy them all and to begin rebuilding a new nation of priests; a nation that would be the light of the world and to the nations of the earth for he remembered his promise to Abraham that through him all the nations of the earth shall be blessed. How could he use a nation of priests that worshipped other gods and embraced idolatry? The Ten Commandments that had been written by the finger of God lay shattered before Moses and the Hebrews. How is it that you cannot keep God's laws, rules and standards? Moses had just received them from God and now they lay at the foot of Mt. Sinai broken and shattered. The irony of it all is that Moses never saw himself as the one who broke the Ten Commandments but as the one who should have enforced them. This tragedy cost them a trip into Canaan – the land flowing with milk and honey and what had been promised to Abraham, Isaac, and Jacob. The very thing that Moses wanted to enforce disqualified him from the promise land and his inheritance.

Oh! This tragic blindness that men hold dear! If Adam only knew half of the headache that he had caused in the garden, he would not have gone near the fruit. What he did was equivalent to gouging our eyes out, then putting us in a large dark room with no windows or light, and asking us to search for a way out of the darkness. It has been this way ever since the fall of men. We are blind men searching for the light when there is no light. We do not know that not only is the room dark and windowless but it will not open from the inside. It must be opened from the outside and there is only one person who holds the key to the door and who can give a blind man light and sight.

So, we stumble in this present darkness with our religion and with our efforts to keep God's laws and commandments. And we do not understand, or know, that there is only one guarantee in our search and in our efforts, and that guarantee is that "WE WILL FAIL."

If God himself does not open the door and let in the light, we will fail. If God himself does not give man back his sight – we will not see and we will not live. We will walk around in our dark rooms forever looking for the door and the light.

By now Korah and Dathan had worked up enough courage to confront Moses about his antics. This was not the way a Levite and priest of God should behave. So, they came. They had no idea that it was the last time that they would see this earth and draw the breath of life. They had no idea that they should have kissed their wives and kids goodbye. God was angry and He was about to show His wrath. It was not what they saw that had landed them in a world of hurt; it was what they didn't see that had driven them off the cliffs into a land of troubles. There was an angry God that not even Moses would be able to placate. What they did not know was that long before now they had stepped over the line and there was no turning back. They should have guessed that something was up when the ground beneath them started to get unusually warm.

"Moses, you have taken too much upon yourself. We are all ministers and priests and God is with us just as much as He is with you. You have dragged us out of our homes in Egypt just so that we would die out here in the wilderness. Moses, we want a piece of the pie and we want a say-so in what is happening to us." Dathan, Abiram, and the other priests chimed in with their sentiments. The wives and children should have started running at this point but they hung around to see if Moses would cave in. He did not.

Moses fell on his face before God. He had been with an angry God and had not been that successful in getting him to turn his fury aside. The wives and children wanted to see Moses get his just rewards for bringing them out of Egypt so they were standing with their husbands grinning from ear to ear. Moses had it coming to him.

Moses yelled out at the crowd that had gathered to see this show. They hadn't chosen their leader yet and as best as they could figure out, whoever came out of this alive would be their leader. Moses cried out to them to separate themselves from Korah and his assembly and some listened and some didn't. They were still clueless as to what was about to happen to them. The congregation now against Moses had reached some twenty thousand with a few thousand sympathizers looking on the scene. As far as the witnesses can remember, they heard a loud deafening clap that sounded like thunder, mixed with a tremendous heat, the earth beneath Korah and his supporters gave way and in less than one minute twenty three thousand people were consumed.[21] The screams and wailing lasted for thirty minutes afterwards. The Hebrews ran for cover and when they had finally recovered from their shock they headed for their tents. It was a devastating blow to Korah and his rebellion. In one day there was a loss of over twenty thousand Hebrew children.

God knows how to deal with rebellion and ambition. When the faithful and newly converted ventured to look out of their tents all that they saw was a giant hole in the ground that had been covered with rocks. Moses had told the congregation that Korah and his men would not die a natural death and his prophecy was now fulfilled. The Hebrews had such a fear of Moses and his God that they began to tremble, hiding in their tents scared that they too might be consumed. Throughout the dark night there was bloodcurdling screams heard throughout the camp because the fire of God was hunting down the rebellious partisans of Korah. Not only were the men consumed by fire but their entire family was eaten by the flames. The Hebrew camp was covered with tears of remorse and sorrow for days, but there were still sympathizers to be hunted and dealt with.

Soon after the darkness finally receded and the morning dawned, the Hebrews of the rebellion became sick and nauseous. There was intense vomiting and a high fever ravaging the people. A plague of cholera, dysentery, and typhoid had landed in the camp and the populace was dropping like flies. Now, the entire settlement, all two millions of them, were concerned and in an uproar. The judgment of God against Korah and the Dathanites was local but this sentence; this pestilence could wipe out all of the people in the Hebrew nation. They came running to Moses because to them it appeared that God was keeping his word to Moses of starting a new nation of priests who would be the light of the world.

The rest of the priests that were left came to Moses with the look of repentance and grief on their face asking him to intercede for

---

[21] 1 Cor. 10:8

them before God because they knew they had no merit before God. They had grumbled at Meribah against Moses and God and they had wanted to go back to Egypt. They had grumbled when there was no food to eat; yet now they walked around Moses with light steps lest they should fall in like the others. They came with their hats in their hands and fear in their hearts; the plague was decimating their numbers but it never came near the tent of Moses. What started out as a peaceful gathering by Eleazar the priest, one of the few that had not been swallowed up, turned very quickly into a mob scene; shouts of stoning were beginning to make their way from the back of this mob of 14,000 people.

But what the mob was too angry to notice, were Moses' eyes. He was totally oblivious to the voices of the horde accusing him of killing the people of God that being Korah, Dathan, and Abiram. Chaos ruled the camp that day; but the more they shouted the more fear there was in Moses' eyes. Aaron was the first one to notice it, and when he did he fell flat on his face. Moses picked him up and whispered into his ear, after which Aaron ran at incredible speed – you would never have seen a 90-year-old man run so fast – towards the tabernacle of God. When he finally got to the temple there was this heavy throbbing noise at the altar of God. It was the sound made when something is about to explode from too much strain and stress. Aaron fell on his face again and began crying out loud to El Shaddai.

In the meantime, the mob had grown to be violent against Moses, and they were clueless as to what was about to happen to them. They never saw the black ominous clouds forming behind them; they never heard the cries of those who had been muffled by the plague that was moving fast behind them and headed their direction at a hurried pace.

The multitude was entirely clueless but angry enough to try killing Moses.

One of the things that is absolutely terrifying about God is that he does not have to announce any of his judgments. Sometimes they

A HUDDLE FOR RIGHTEOUSNESS

come without warning but they come. Moses knew what was about to happen to the mob that had assembled against God's leader of the Hebrews.

Before Aaron could make atonement for the sins of the people, over 14,000 Hebrews had joined Korah in Hades. It happened in an instant. Bodies were laid low in forty-five different directions. The Hebrew's were being destroyed until Aaron finished interceding on their behalf. And when he finally returned to Moses the curse of death was lifted. Both men, Moses and Aaron, returned to their tents and wept.

This God is holy! The curse of Adam on the descendants of Adam was lethal. It had laid waste another 14,000 people in one day. Those poor lost souls never knew what hit them, but now that they were in Hades they had full knowledge. Adam in his decision to eat the fruit that was forbidden cursed man in countless ways that would bring about his physical and spiritual death. The Hebrews who did not understand God believed that they could change his agenda to suit their own. They believed that they could sway the hand of God at their own choosing and had to learn the hard way. It was a game that they played. It was a game that cost them their life.

One of the prophets looked out and mourned over the dead bodies and said, "My people are dead from the lack of knowledge." Today at the foot of Sinai a very powerful lesson had been learned by the Hebrews. God does not play games. The stakes are too high. The school of hard knocks was open for the Hebrews and He was still demanding that they pay tuition.

When Aaron went back into the tabernacle, it was silent, the plague had been lifted from the Hebrew camp and those who were opposing Moses were fast being eliminated, for now at least there were a few moments of rest in the settlement. He took a moment to reflect on his own life for he was by no means a righteous man. He had used the gift that God had given to him to make a golden calf to be idolized and worshipped by the Hebrews. Would God also be angry with him? Would God also destroy him along with the rebellious ones of Korah? Or were there other issues of righteousness and right living at stake?

The psalmist addresses the issues of righteousness and the sovereignty of God, when he says, "Why do the heathen rage against God and the man of God? Why be foolish enough to imagine that you can turn His hand away. It is a vanity. Such as the rebellious plot against the King and abide the counsel against His anointed one, saying let us break the yoke of bondage that He has placed on us; let us throw away His system of government and His rule over us. Then God will sit in the heaven and laugh, it will echo throughout the universe and it will be heard by all. In the middle of his laughter He is saying, *'I will have them in derision and division.'*"

His expression then changes. His eyebrows become narrow and his jaw is set as he says, "I have set my anointed one upon my holy hill of Zion and no one shall move him. This is my chosen one and I have brought him forth." The psalmist then proceeds to warn the rebellious ones that God is in His element and that it is not good for one to bring folly before the Lord of host.

Kiss the King! Oh ye people lest he becomes angry and rises up against you. Do homage to his anointed one while the wrath of God is kindled but a little while unless you perish by the way. At the foot of Sinai, God's wrath was kindled until Aaron kissed the King. Could the issues of righteousness and righteous living have a lot to do with God's choice in being righteous and holy before him? Men too often confuse keeping holy standards as being righteous and pleasing to God and this causes them to miss the issues completely. It has been a part of the psyche of man ever since Adam fell and Cain raised his fist to the face of God. Man wants to do things his way and sooner or later God accommodates him. He has given to us the awesome power of choosing our destinies for this life and the afterlife. It is all too often the case that after man has chosen his destiny that he blames God for his failures, when it is he who has exercised his own free will.

This would be the case with Moses who had also stepped over the line in the wilderness. He had chosen his own destiny. His long and difficult battles with the Hebrews had cost him dearly in his pilgrimage. He had been trained for over forty years for this moment and he was not able to fulfill the plan of God. He could see his destination from a distance, he could almost reach out and touch it but it might as well have been a million miles away from him. Forty years in Egypt, forty years of training as a desert shepherd, but he would not see his goals reached. He had made a fundamental error in his relationship with God.

So one day, God called him aside and spoke to the embattled leader. Moses knew that the meeting was not going to be that good. The serious tone of the meeting left him with an empty feeling in his stomach and that feeling was justified. There, on the side of a rugged mountain in the Midian desert, he wept bitterly. He pleaded with God to once again change his mind and to give him another chance. The pleading went unheeded. Moses had botched the opportunity of a lifetime simply because he had repeated the same mistake that he made in Egypt over 80 years ago. He had stepped in front of God to take the lead. It was a colossal mistake that caused him to take the life of a man and be labeled a murderer. He had not learned the lessons from Egypt. The tears began to flow down the face of Moses because he knew that God had given him the opportunity of a lifetime and because he could not control his anger it cost him a great price. He fell on his face before God but a stern unyielding voice told him that he would be replaced by Joshua. In those brief moments Moses' mind drifted back to Meribah where the Hebrew's were once again griping and complaining about food and water and wanting to go back to Egypt. By this time Moses had reached his short limit and his blood was boiling hot. God spoke to Moses in the heat of his passion but he only heard a portion of what God had said.

The congregation there in the wilderness had assembled before a huge rock there in the Midian desert. It was to be a defining moment for God to explain and demonstrate who he was and what he could do for his people. Moses did not see it that way and once again he stepped in front of God and went wayward of his plan. Instead of speaking to the rock as God had very plainly commanded him, he took his rod and struck the image that God wanted to give to the people. It was an affront to God and God took it as such. Moses walked up to the rock and raised his rod over his head in the air.

"Shall I bring water from this rock you rebellious people?" Moses struck the rock twice and water came forth in abundance for the assembly. There was one big problem; Moses after he had struck the rock twice; he was now in big trouble with God again. God wanted his image and his power on display and not those of Moses. That is why he clearly commanded him to speak to the rock and not to strike it.

When Moses struck the rock he destroyed the image that God wanted to give to the Hebrews and replaced it with himself. He would now be seen as their provider and not God.

In the meantime back on the side of the mountain Moses looks into the stern face of God and hears the words that crush him. "Moses, you are disqualified. Take a look at the land that is flowing with milk and honey because you will never be able to go to Canaan. Joshua will take your place and lead my people in the promised-land." It was more than Moses could bear. His whole world was crashing in around him. He had lived and dreamed for this moment for over 40 years and now that he was only a mile from the land that was flowing with milk and honey, he might as well be a thousand miles away. It was so close and yet so far away. The very thing that he had so long tried to enforce had cost him a trip into the promised-land. God left him to be alone and to think over his costly mistake and error. Surely there must be a better way to be made righteous and holy before the living God; for men cannot hold to commandment and regulations. Is it possible for a man who was a murderer in his past to be made righteous before a holy God? Would his murder of the Egyptian soldier cost him a trip to heaven? Surely God has provided for there to be a sacrifice to substitute for the sins of man. For the first time in his life his confidence had taken flight. As a general in the Egyptian army he commanded thousands and conquered entire nations, but somehow in the realm of the spirit none of his fleshly abilities mattered much. It was dark on the side of the mountain that day. Moses realized after his disqualification from the promised-land that he was no better than the people that he was trying to lead to the promised-land because they had all been disqualified by God. They would all perish in the desert wilderness which was forty miles from the promised-land. Though their clothes did not wear out nor did their shoes wear down, you did see a tombstone on a daily basis.

Many times they had tried to enter into the promised-land on their own without God's help but the games they had played in the wilderness with God had disqualified them. Every time they tried to cross over, an avenging army would come down on them and chase them back into the wilderness. They could see it, they could taste it, they could smell it, but they could not cross over to go and live there.

Moses then sent for Joshua to tell him the good news and the bad. Joshua would be their new leader who would take them into the promised-land but he, Moses, would not be going with them. The people gave him promises of how they would be determined to keep the laws of God in the new land of milk and honey, but he knew differently, for they had given him to the same promises early on at Horeb. So, God gave them a promise through Moses when he said, "They have spoken well therefore I will raise up a prophet from among them like unto you Moses, and I will put my words into his mouth. They did not listen to you Moses but to him they will listen."[22]

It was a cloudy gloomy day for the embattled leader of the Hebrews. The dark clouds overhead were a premonition of the things to come for Moses. That day he was to have a private meeting with the Commander in chief before they were to leave for the promise land. He did not have a good feeling about this heart to heart talk with God. He looked at the mountains where God was waiting for him and he began to shuffle his feet back and forth as he kicked a few stones around in the dirt. He began to review the things that he had done wrong and tried to bolster his confidence with the things that he had done right in order to prepare himself for his argument with God.

His conscience took him back to the Egyptian soldier that he had hidden in the sand; would God still be angry with him even after all

---

[22] Deut. 18:15

that he had done to deliver his people out of Egypt. He had a bad feeling about this meeting and thought about skipping out altogether so that he would not have to suffer the confrontation. Fear gripped his heart like never before as he took his first steps up the mountain. The closer he got to his destination the slower his steps became in that he was trying to put off the inevitable.

Halfway there, the journey was too much for the eighty year old. He fell on his face and began pleading with God to give him one more chance to get it right. There was a cold and lonely silence. He prayed again with the same fervency and intercession that had stopped God from wiping out an entire nation of Hebrews. Moses was in trouble and he knew it. The suspense was killing him. The heavens were as silent as the night sky and it was never this way with Moses before because God had always spoken face to face with him. God was angry with Moses! And he was going forward to face the consequences. Zipporah eyes began to tear up as she saw her courageous husband go to his meeting with God. She also had a gut feeling that things would not go well for her husband of these many years. After eighty some years in the Lord's service Moses was now seeing a face of God that he did not recognize.

The men and women below who had supported Moses reached out to him in support but nothing could be done, he had to face this trial alone. They quickly began gathering their possessions because they had known of no one else who would stand in the gap for them before God like Moses. Just as he was about to reach the top of Mount Nebo the ground shook from the sound of a heavy voice and Moses immediately recognized who it was.

"Moses!" There was as sternness in the tone of this heavy voice. Moses began trembling at the knees as his confidence was now shredded. He had seen what this God could do to those who did not keep his law and his commandments and to those who rebelled against him. "Moses do not pray again and petition me to go into the promise land anymore for you will not see the land that I swore to your forefathers Abraham, Isaac, and Jacob. Your rebellion against my commandments at Meribah has disqualified you from entering into the land flowing with milk and honey.[23]

If Moses had been a man of lesser stature and strength his heart would have failed him for this is what he had been looking for and had left the Midian desert for. He had waited for forty years and had trained for another forty just to reach this point and now he could go no further. The two old friends were walking together to the top of Mt. Pisgah so that Moses could at least get a look at the land that he had so long waited to see and to be a part of. He looked to the East, the West, the North and the South and then he looked down at his feet and wept. Once more he looked into the face of his friend to see if he would find mercy but he did not. The incident at Meribah was of a very serious offense in the sight of God. His friend left him there on Mt Pisgah after he had reassured him that Joshua would take the people of God into Canaan over the Jordan River. He made his way back down to find Joshua and the people all packed, and ready to go; knowing that he would never see them again. The two men hugged each other for the last time and looked for each other as long as they could before the final parting.

Joshua took his place front and center of this new generation of Hebrews that had left the old to die in the wilderness. He was God's choice to lead them into the land flowing with milk and honey along with his friend Caleb. They were men of faith and they were the ones who stood tall when they came back with a report from the land of Canaan. They were the only two of the group of scouts that said that they could go in and take the land. The other scouts reported that the Nephalim were in the land and that they were giants in comparison to the Hebrews but Joshua and Caleb were not deterred. When this new generation finally entered into the land they quickly realized that it was occupied; and that they would have to drive out the inhabitants by force. The Nephalim were none to happy about this situation and it took a little convincing to remove them seeing that they were the ancestors of Goliath. Nevertheless, they had heard through the grapevine that the Hebrew's were coming by some Egyptians who

---

[23] Numbers 27:14

were fishing at the Red Sea when the Egyptian army decided to cross over and go after the Hebrews. So they knew reputation of the Hebrew God.

The wells that were already dug; the land that was already cultivated, the fruit trees that were already planted were well guarded by nine foot men who were fierce in the protection of their land, but inside their hearts they trembled with fear because of the God of the Hebrews. The land was theirs for the taking but it would have to be done by faith and with a fight. They needed God's help. They needed to live such a life of righteousness and faith before God that they could take their inheritance from the Nephalim who were the giants of the land for the righteous man shall live by faith. Was this the mistake of their forefathers at Kadesh-Barnea and in the wilderness? Was this the reason that they were disqualified along with Moses in the desert? What was this new life of righteousness all about?

Moses watched as Joshua led the Hebrews into the land flowing with milk and honey and soon after Moses slept but he did not rest. He knew that one day his prophecy would come true and that even though they would not listen to him one day one was coming to whom they would listen

Chapter Eight

**THE NEW MOSES
AND THE RIGHTEOUS LIFE**

She stumbled into the little white steeple church at the end of the road with blood shot eyes that hid a heart that was screaming for help. Staggering through the front door; she was looking for something or for someone. The preacher saw her first and was happy that someone new had come into his congregation after all his efforts of door to door evangelism. Yet this was not exactly what he wanted to see. The expression on his face quickly changed from a smile to a scowl and then to utter embarrassment. He stuttered through the rest of the sermon and the congregation, all fifteen of them, quickly realized that something was wrong. They looked around curiously to find out what was making the preacher so upset. They quickly spotted the culprit.

There she was huddled over in the corner all by herself with her head down and weeping and praying so that no one would discover her. She had come into the church, the little sanctified, Holy Ghost, hell fire, and damnation preaching church of God drunk as a skunk. And a skunk is precisely what she smelled and looked like. She reeked of liquor. Well, that just about did it for the Holy Ghost, hell fire, and damnation preaching little church, at the end of the road. The preacher upped his rhetoric and his tone of voice figuring that this would scare her out of hell and alcohol, but all to no avail. She wouldn't be sober for a couple of months to come, and maybe that wasn't so bad after all; seeing that all the hell fire and damnation preaching was aimed directly at her. As after every chant and threat from the preacher received a hearty 'Amen' from the congregation (all fifteen) as they picked up on the spirit of condemnation that was now flooding the church.

How could she? How could she have the gall to come into God's holy, sanctified, hellfire and damnation preaching church on a Sunday morning as drunk as a skunk and twice as smelly? Actually, she wasn't the first one to ever look or act like this, because Sister Johnson with the big bowl of fruit hat on top of her head, would have to wake herself up from the head bobbing back and forth on Sunday morning to keep everyone from hearing her snore so loud during the hell fire and brimstone sermons of Rev. Blanton and the "couldn't carry a tune if it was in a bucket" singing of the preacher's wife.

That day the church at the end of the dirt road did one of the most horrible things that you could ever do to a person. They completely ignored her and treated her as if she was nothing more than part of the furnishings of the church. They stared at her with every chance they had as if she was a leper that had just recently escaped from the colony. That wasn't the worst of it, after the service no one spoke or greeted her. They went out of their way to avoid this sinner-woman. This young lady of the night needed that like she needed a hole in the head. All that she could do at this time was hold her head down against the back of the pew, and wait until everyone had filed out of this hell fire and damnation preaching church. Not even the pastor would minister to her but quickly walked past her to greet the holy and righteous members of his congregation hoping that she would leave his holy little church never to return again.

Marie had come to church that day looking for help. No one there needed to tell her that she was a sinner in need of the grace of God, and indeed that was not what she would find at the little church at the end of the road. You would have thought that she was carrying the Bubonic plague all over again. She staggered out of the church alone that afternoon as the holy sanctified church members looked down at the ground as she stumbled passed them on her way home. Was this what God was all about? If so, she wanted nothing more to do with him. She was finding this kind of treatment outside of the church and she surely didn't want to go back into the church if this was the attitude they had towards her.

When Marie left the church that day she was a lot worse off than when she came in looking for help. It was always her philosophy that the church was like a hospital for sick people to go and get well, but in this place there were no sick people. Everyone was healthy, holy, and righteous and frowned upon the unhealthy, the unholy, and the unrighteous. Marie staggered to her car fumbled for the keys, and tried to pretend that this event had never happened in her life. Was there any place on earth where she could find help and a solution to her problems? Was there any place on earth where you could go to let the wounds from the world around you heal. She went back home to her three kids and to the only friend she knew that would accept her unconditionally – the bottle. She would be intoxicated for some time to come.

She lay on her bed that night and looked up at the stars thinking and half way praying because she didn't know if God answered the prayers of such a sinner as herself. Marie asked God if there was a better way to get to know him as opposed to the humiliation and condemnation that she had received from the little church at the end of the road. She quickly fell asleep after another bottle of Kentucky whiskey and in her dreams there appeared a man that she had read about only as a child in Sunday school. He too was preaching hell fire and damnation and he had two tablets of stone in his hands, and a long finger pointed out towards a ragged and wicked looking congregation.

"Blessed shall you be in the city if you obey God's law. Blessed shall you be in the country if you keep God's word. Blessed shall be in your going out and in your coming in, if you keep the covenants of God, and cursed is everyone who does not keep the law of God." His face began to shine like the sun as if he was being **transformed** in his sermon on the mount and as he continued his blessings, "Blessed are the pure in heart for they shall see God. Blessed are those that mourn for they shall be comforted, blessed are you when men say all evil against you falsely, rejoice and be glad for great is your reward in heaven. In your walk with God, be perfect as your heavenly Father is perfect." And the man from Galilee left with his disciples following closely after him.

Marie in her dream wanted very much to be a disciple of Jesus, but she did not understand what he meant when he told her to be perfect as your heavenly Father is perfect. How can anyone be perfect before a holy and righteous God? It is impossible. Most of the people starring at him were imperfect and sinners. John the Baptist had spread the word that they needed to repent and turn to the Messiah. But there was something unique and different about this new Messiah. He showed compassion and tenderness to the flock. It infuriated the religious leaders of that day who wanted to hold a tight line over the masses, and who preached hell fire, brimstone, and condemnation. Jesus was different.

Chapter Nine

When Jesus came down off the mountain he did not find a golden calf in the midst of the congregation, but he did find something that was much worse; a hard, rigid, corrupt religious system that would plague him throughout his ministry and ultimately be the cause of his death. The religious of that day followed his every move, listened to his every word, and tried every way known to man to trap and trip him. They were the descendents of Korah who antagonized Moses in the wilderness and now they were after the New Moses with a vengeance. A deep-seated hatred formed in them because this man was becoming a threat to their system, their way of life, but most of all their money. That day the disciples followed Jesus into the wilderness and soon the crowd that had followed him began to grow weak and weary from the lack of food. They witnessed the same hunger and thirst as their predecessors but this time the rock that followed them had become flesh and blood. When his disciples pressed him for food and water he told them to feed the crowd themselves. After they had restored some semblance of order Jesus fed over five thousand people that day from a few loaves of bread and a few fish. The disciples gathered the twelve loads of bread and sat down with Jesus to have a talk about what had happened. Some had begun to discuss the similarities as to what had happened to their fathers in the wilderness and how they were given manna to eat that sustained their physical life. So they came to Jesus just as their fathers did looking for more manna and more food from Jesus. But Jesus knew their hearts and did not open himself up to them. Some of the Jews were coming to take him by force and to make him the King of Israel but Jesus did not give himself to them. When they came looking for him to continually fill their bellies Jesus told them of what had happened in the wilderness. It was not Moses who gave the manna but it was God in heaven who had given their fore-fathers food to replete their belly.

Well, Jesus was doing fairly well in the opinion polls of that day until he made his next comment. He said, "I am the bread of life, I am the manna from heaven that has been sent by the Father. He who eats of my flesh shall never hunger again." That did it for about 40 or 50 of his disciples. This was more than they could take. They didn't mind the fish and bread but cannibalism was a bit too much for them to bear so they left. Jesus then turned to the remaining disciples and said, "Will you leave me also?" Peter stepped up without thinking and spoke (which is his trademark, foot-in-mouth disease), and said: "Lord, where shall we go, you alone have the answers to eternal life." Peter did have foot-in-mouth disease but every once in a while he got it right.

The Sons of Korah began beating the war drums again. "Isn't this man the son of Joseph the carpenter? How can he promise to give us life when he is a mere man himself?" How can he make claims that he has been sent by the Father to give us eternal life?" It was all about to boil to a head. They were as blind as their forefathers in the wilderness who had also ignored the miracles from God. All of that meant nothing to them; they wanted what they wanted and when they wanted it. Their focus was on the here-and-now and not the thereafter. So it was with the sons of Korah. They couldn't have cared less about the spiritual significance of Jesus *being* the manna that came down from heaven. They wanted full stomachs for themselves and their children. They literally missed the opportunity of a lifetime with this new Moses that had come upon the scene.

It began in the month of September around the fifteenth and lasted for one week. Jerusalem was littered with what looked like Bedouin tents that spread all over the city so as to surround the temple. It was every man's solemn duty to come and participate on this momentous occasion. The feast of booths commemorated the wilderness dwellings of their forefathers as they were being led by Moses, and once again the sons of Korah were spoiling for a bloody nose. They were of the few ministers of that day who actually set out to murder people. They set the traps and laid the plans to get rid of this pesky fellow from Galilee that was undercutting their authority. He simply had to go; Jerusalem was not large enough for him, his doctrine, and the doctrine of the scribes and Pharisees.

So, Jesus knowing this; decided to wait until the middle of the feast before venturing in and teaching. He came to the temple and the crowd dogged his every step. Whenever he had finished his teachings to the people there was nearly always a riot or a revival. Some believed him and called him the prophet of which, Moses had spoken that was yet to come[24]. They had seen the power of the miracles and put two and two together. However, the sons of Korah had other motives behind their words and actions. They wanted Jesus dead. They wanted him out of their hair. So there were great debates in the streets of Jerusalem after he had spoken to his people. Those who spoke of Jesus as being the prophet did so quietly for fear of the Jewish leadership who hated Jesus. Nevertheless, after every sermon that Jesus preached, he was gathering a throng of followers, an enormous throng at that. This unnerved the religious leaders of the day who had failed in their initial attempt to kill him[25]. They were indeed a brood of vipers that had little to offer to the people of Jerusalem of that day. They robbed them of their money in the pretense of doing the work of God. On the other hand, Jesus very quietly set up shop in the corner of the temple and did not take center stage away from the religious leaders. However, he knew, along with all of Jerusalem, that a showdown was brewing because there was a fire being lit under the leadership, and the fire was getting hotter and hotter as the days went by. The pilgrims that came to Jerusalem year after year were being drawn to this young prophet from Galilee.

Whenever the crowds pressed him to the point where he could not move, he spoke to them, telling them about the Kingdom of God. The ears that listened to him brought joy to the heart of some and fostered conspiracy in the heart of others. The common folks received him gladly but the sons of Korah wanted nothing more than to put him in prison and from there to quietly kill him which had

---

[24] John 7:40
[25] John 7:25

been the fate of several want-to-be messiahs before Jesus. Jesus on many occasions confronted them plainly and asked them why they were trying to kill him. And to the surprise of the crowd they had no answer. The more they persecuted him the more his popularity grew until the religious leaders could not take it any more. They sent officers to take him and to put him in prison but the officers failed in their attempts especially after they had heard what he had to say. The Spirit bore witness in their hearts that Jesus was the Messiah and that he was the Prophet of which Moses had spoken.

It frustrated the religious leaders to no end, so they met with one idea in mind and that was to eliminate Jesus Christ. No one stopped to ask if Moses had said, "Thou shalt not kill," or whether or not they were keeping the Commandments of Moses by going around killing people. If you keep the law why not read your law book every nine or ten years or so – it just might have been very helpful in their decision making process. That, of course, never occurred to them. By day they paraded around as priests and ministers but by night it was a totally different matter. So they met secretly with only one who was in opposition to their plans; and that was Nicodemus[26]. They very quickly overrode his vote and proceeded with their conspiracy. The leader of this group was Caiaphus. He had failed so often in his attempts to end Jesus life that he knew he needed a special plan in order to trap him. The priests that he had sent previously to entrap Jesus had been blown away and embarrassed, so he decided to use the same technique that Satan had used when he had tempted Jesus on the mountain. He would use the Scriptures to entrap him.

Now Caiaphus knew from early encounters with Jesus that he and his priests were way over their head when they wanted to use the Scriptures to catch him in political suicide. So they met and prayed about another plan. Whatever it was it had to be good, it had to be right in their eyes, and in its employment Jesus would need to destroy his credibility before the eyes of the people. So after their prayer, Caiaphus came up with an idea; a brilliant, devious plan that was a surefire winner.

---

[26] John 7:50,51

A HUDDLE FOR RIGHTEOUSNESS

He had been familiar along with his priests with a young lady who had come up to celebrate the feasts of booths. She was estranged from her husband even though they were married at age 12. She had come to the priests many, many times searching for answers and searching for help. She found neither. She was born and raised in the region of Magdela and had come to Jerusalem with her religious but absent husband. The priest who gave her help gave her the wrong kind of help. The ministers who comforted her gave the wrong kind of comfort and she had decided to be none the wiser for it. It would be used as punishment against her husband who was abusive.

Caiaphus knew where she and her husband resided every year. The people of the feast usually came early to put up their tents and picked the best places knowing that it would be a very long seven days in a tent. The Magdalene woman was there with her kids as usual and she would now become a pawn in the hands of the scribes and Pharisees to use against Jesus. The conspiracy had been meticulously thought out in advance. The trap door was all but shut on Jesus; now all they needed was the bait and for Jesus to take the bait.

It was about mid-afternoon on the next to the last day of the feast. The woman from Magdela was about to receive her customer as she had put her kids out to play with the others. She knew her customer well from previous encounters and she received him with mixed emotions. He was one of the members of the temple. The priest who had set the trap waited precisely for the right moment of exposure so as to say that they were eyewitnesses of the adulterous affair. And like clockwork they came and caught the surprised couple in the midst of the act. They grabbed the woman from Magdela and carried her to where Jesus was teaching, but surprisingly so her partner escaped from this incident unharmed in body and in reputation. He made off better than a cat burglar in a jewelry store. Those who kept the law were selectively enforcing the law. According to the law both parties are equally guilty[27] and both parties were to be judged,

---

[27] Leviticus 20:10

but there was no sign of her partner nor was there evidence that the law was being enforced properly. The law keepers were proving to be lawbreakers who could not keep or enforce the law[28] but on the outside things looked the same.

Now Jesus had just come into the temple from the Mount of Olives and probably it was not the best time to spring a trap on him. There were hundreds of people who had crowded in around him to hear his teachings. The scribes and Pharisees were licking their chops and rubbing their hands together. It could not have been a more perfect setting – Jesus' teaching regarding leniency under the law would be put to a major test. He was about to be discredited before all of Jerusalem. His teachings would not be adhered to by anyone. If he supported the death penalty for adultery in those days, he would have just discredited what he had taught the multitude there in the temple about the grace and goodness of his father. It was a-lose-lose situation for Jesus Christ and the Pharisees knew it. They were absolutely convinced that they would once and for all be rid of Jesus.

They dragged Mary Magdalene through the streets and towards the temple like a rag doll in the hands of a two-year-old. If she had wanted secrecy she surely did not have it now because the crowd in the streets began to sense that something big was in the air. They followed the scribes and Pharisees all the way to the temple. They knew that someone had committed a capital offense and there was going to be an execution. The poor, helpless woman at the end of the rope was pulled into the temple kicking and screaming and knowing that she would never see the light of day again. Would these priests of God kill this woman in the temple of God? Many in the crowd including the scribes and Pharisees had picked up rocks along the way in expectation of executing this woman from Magdela. In her mind she knew that she was guilty but so were the priests who had been with her on several occasions. During this era women were property and men treated them just about any way they chose; which

---

[28] Romans 2:17-29

A HUDDLE FOR RIGHTEOUSNESS

is the reason for the priests getting away with stoning her after having slept with her.

The woman from Magdela wore a brazen look on her face from the years of abuse from the men in her life and this last treachery was just one more in a long series of disappointments. Her bronzed skin had long years of trials and heartache written throughout. She was all too happy to leave this earth and her miserable fate with it. The brazen look soon turned into a defiant stare as if she was looking right through the men who had her on the other end of a rope. Her husband did not plead her case or plead for her life as he himself was afraid of the power of the Pharisees. They had the authority to throw you out of the synagogue and that would be devastating. It was the same as committing someone to the pits of hell. So, the lady from Magdela stood alone battered, bruised, and half naked from her dragging through the streets at the end of a rope. It was the end of a long life of failures and poor decisions on Mary of Magdela's part. She stood before the crowd exposed but, strangely enough, at this moment, her back began to stiffen and her fears were being replaced with dignity. She knew that the men who had placed her against the wall for execution were just as guilty as she. So what was the need to leave this world in fear and shame? Her jaw was set and her chin came forward as for the first time she looked into the eyes of her accusers and what she saw in these eyes both enraged and emboldened her. She saw guilt. They were just as guilty as she but they had been more successful in covering it up. She was the one who just happened to be caught. She looked up again as they pulled her in front of this strange looking rabbi that she had never heard of or had been with. In her mind they were on trial for the sins that they had committed but just had not been revealed. The sons of Korah were hiding behind their religion again. Their system of righteousness was no better than the code that she had lived by. So who gave them the right to judge her? If they had broken the law they were supposed to enforce then they were twice as guilty as she. When she looked around her she not only saw hypocrisy but blindness. How could a just and righteous God allow this to happen to her at the hands of men who were just as guilty, if not more so, than she was.

With her brazen face she gazed into the faces of the crowd which was in the hundreds by now, her eyes returned to the one young rabbi who was standing in the corner of the temple teaching. His eyes were different; they did not condemn her like the rest and she fixed her gaze on his as she would have a bit of comfort at least as she left this world. When she looked at him she did see judgment but it was not a judgment that brought condemnation. It was a judgment of knowing her. She had never heard of this bold young rabbi traveling the countryside who had taken on the religious system of that day and how he had called them into account for their lifestyle. It was told her that he had rightly so labeled them hypocrites who had logs in their eyes but were walking around trying to take splinters out of the eyes of the congregation. If this was so then he had aptly described the scribes and Pharisees of that day. Mary was a whipping post for the guilt that was in them.

She came face to face with the rabbi from Galilee and listened in to the lies they proffered to him. Caiaphus was the first to start in on Jesus.

"Master, this woman was caught in the very act of adultery. What should we do with this sinner woman? Moses says to stone her. What do you say?"

Caiaphus was no dummy. He had not arrived at his position by default. His scheme would put Jesus up against the wall and both men knew it. He was right in his partial and selective interpretation of Scripture and his application of it. The bottom line of this encounter against Jesus was that the accusers of this lady were absolutely correct. There was no error in their interpretation of Leviticus or in their carrying it out. They had learned their lessons from the other encounters with Jesus that he had not subjected himself to their customs and 'make up laws as you go' routines. If they were going to trap Jesus they would have to be correct in their use of the Scriptures or they would be blown out of the water as they had been so many times before. So this time Caiaphus felt good about the trap that he had laid for this new rabbi.

Often times, I think we must be amusing to God by some of the things that we try and pull off. There were hundreds and hundreds of people surrounding Jesus, the scribes and Pharisees by this time; and God must have been delighted at the opportunity to get his message across to the people regarding living a righteous life. The stage was set for this tremendous showdown. One would walk away a winner the other with a sore butt.

Solomon addressed those who lay traps for their unsuspecting victims rightfully; he said *"they lie in wait for their own blood."*

Jesus took his time in answering their questions knowing a trap had been set for him. He bent down to the ground at the knees and begins to write with his fingers on the ground. No one knew exactly what the Aramaic said but it sure did cause a lot of speculation. More than anything it gave everyone a chance to think before they acted, especially the *self-righteous* religious leaders of that day.

The old Moses was an old wine skin bursting at the seams and leaking over; straining to do its very best to handle the new wine poured into it but all to no avail. In the end neither the wine nor the wineskin was preserved and both were lost.[29] The old Moses was doomed for failure in his effort to contain the new wine of Jesus Christ and the work of the Holy Spirit in this new dispensation that Jesus was and is bringing into the nation of Israel. The old laws of Moses are like old garments[30] being patched together because of the tears that it has suffered. No one puts a new cloth on an old tear because the latter tear would become even worse than the original. No – you throw out the old garments and get brand new ones. Jesus knew this when he confronted the sons of Korah of that day. He had been given new garments by God to give to the people of God; and those were garments of righteousness.

The old Moses is a near sighted doctor that can only see the symptoms of his patients and who can only diagnose the disease.

---

[29] Matt 9:17
[30] Matt 9:16

He is good at giving out prescriptions but poor in the healing process. He is not equipped to deal with real problems or the source of the disease. He was never meant to do so; therefore all that he can do is pass out aspirins for those of us who have cancer. It is a temporary and pitiable solution at best. It only postpones the inevitable. You see many of these prescriptions being handed out on Sunday mornings from the pulpit but you and I both know they only last until we can make our way out of the back door of the church. Thus, we have need for the new Moses who can deal with the source of our problems and who can do radical and life saving surgery on the human soul.[31] Radical surgery is needed! A radical soul saving lobotomy is in order!

Six inches of life saving surgery from the ear to the human soul was needed to deal with the source of man's problems and only Jesus could perform it.

Moses had a fundamental problem in his relationship with men and his problem was universal and Jesus knew this as he pondered how to answer these men. He knew that Moses and the law was not the answer to the problems of man nor would he ever be able to deal with the complexities of the human psyche. He was never meant to do so. Moses was an administrative and judicial entity and that was not what the human race needed. The human race begs for Moses to be dropped in flesh and blood and that is exactly who and what Jesus Christ was. He was Moses in flesh and blood, skin and bones and with the ability to identify with man.

Moses could not have done that. He was impersonal and mechanical. He was a judge not a God but on this day he was a substitute for the living God. In his Sermon on the Mount Jesus had told the Pharisees that he who looks upon a woman for lust had already committed the same crime as the adulterous woman. He got at the true essence of what Moses was all about; 'being righteous at heart and before God.' The sons of Korah were hypocritical in their judgment because the law makes hypocrites of us all and Jesus

---

[31] Psalm 40:6, Hebrews 4:12

knew this. He was the new sheriff in town and he wanted to bring in a new law.

There was a precious life in front of him that was about to be taken and all the Pharisees saw was a law that had been violated and not a person. They, much like Moses, did not see the inside of a person but merely looked at the outside and judged the symptoms. They were inadequate judges of human nature that knew not the heart of man but stood to advance their own agenda in order to keep their pockets full. Jesus saw more than a law that had been violated. He saw a person; something much more valuable than the world itself. He came to elevate men and women above the law and to tell the world that your system is not more important than your souls; that the religious process is not more important than the person. Moses was inadequate now, he was fading fast like the snows of summer, and as the scribe and Pharisees were about to find out the hard way. The eyes that looked at the condemned woman were full of compassion and understanding. Now there were only about 800 people standing around and waiting for Jesus to answer the question and he was not about to disappoint anyone.

He stood toe-to-toe with these hardliners, looked them in the eye and said something that brought the house down in that day. "Let him who is without sin among you be the first to cast a stone at her."

He stooped down on the ground and waited for the flying rocks and to hear the screams of a person being executed. You could have heard a pen drop but all you saw were looks of confusion and embarrassment. They knew exactly what he meant, and they knew that he knew. The one who cast the first stone would be her primary accuser and the person who had the ability to be her judge. When Jesus said '*let him who is without sin cast the first stone*', he could not have meant that the judging person had to be sinless on all facets of his life in order to be qualified to make a judgment on this woman or else it would invalidate all of his commands that he gave to Moses. He did not come to do away with the law he came to fulfill the Law of Moses. So the very sin that he mentioned here had to do with the sin of adultery itself. These sons of Korah had committed adultery with this woman or with others as well probably.

Later on he took them to task and called them whitewashed tombs that were full of dead bones and all kinds of corruption. It is of no wonder that they wanted to kill Jesus. He exposed them for what they really were. They were guilty of the same crime that they were accusing this woman, and the only difference between Mary and the Pharisees was their position in society. The rocks that they held so tight in their hands were now dropping to the ground where they belonged in the first place. They didn't know whether to spit or whistle. Around 800 sets of eyes watched as the scribes and Pharisees crawled back into the hole from whence they came. Oh, how they hated Jesus with a passion and instead of going home to figure out if he was right or wrong they went home to stew and fret and to lick their wounds a bit. It never occurred to them that Jesus was right; they wanted him dead, so that they would get on with being righteous and holy after they had murdered him in cold blood. The show had to go on at all cost.

The crowds that surrounded Jesus had a new hero because many of them were in the very same shoes as this woman and wondering what would happen to them. Their faces that were full of fear now had hope because of what they had just witnessed. It was a story to be told to their children's children. Jesus had humiliated their oppressors and had given them new hope and a reason for living. After much prayer some of the Pharisees, mainly Joseph and Nicodemus, came up with answers as to why their colleagues had just returned from an engagement with Jesus with their tails dragging between their legs.

If their interpretation was correct and their application of the law was correct, what was it that went wrong in Caiaphus' well-thought out scheme? It occurred to Nicodemus that the sons of Korah were right about the letter of the law but were wrong in the spirit of the law[32]. Behind every law and every commandment there beats the kind and gracious heart of a loving God who is more interested in having a relationship with his people than he is in them keeping

---

[32] 1Cor 3:6

46,000 rules and regulations. At the end of the Torah there is almost a disclaimer by Moses in Deuteronomy 27. He pronounces a curse on anyone who is not able to keep the whole law written in the Torah, now that is a fairly tall order seeing that there are hundreds and hundreds of laws to keep. It is not possible to keep the law[33]. It never has been possible to live by Moses and the prophets and it never will be possible.

The Sabbath has been made for man and not vice versa. The frail human being has been made for a relationship not for the keeping of laws and covenants that make liars of us all. The sons of Korah never got the idea nor did they want to – they were interested in their position and in their wallets and in the end they would meet the same fate as their forefathers in the wilderness. They knew the letter but not the Spirit. It all came flooding back to Nicodemus; the reason that Jesus had made them so angry when he repeatedly asked them if they had ever read the books of the Torah. They were infuriated and insulted because they had read it to the point of knowing how many letters were in a line and in a book, but what Jesus was really telling them is that if they did not understand the spirit of the law that they could not know the Spirit who gave them the law. If they did not understand who gave them the law then they did not know God. The sons of Korah were clueless when it came to knowing God, and so they were trying to tell the people of Israel about someone that they themselves knew nothing about. It was the blind leading the blind and both falling into the ditch.

Well, it goes without saying that Jesus had really won a place of affection in the hearts of the sons of Korah. They had his picture on the walls and really spoke kindly of him towards one another. They just couldn't wait to see him again, but for now they had to wait until the knots on their head cooled off a bit. Jesus had left some whelps on them and they really intended to return the favor.

Jesus waited until the last snake had slithered back into his hole, and then he went over to the woman from Magdela. She didn't quite know what to expect from her new accuser or liberator. But it was

---

[33] Galatians 3:11

his eyes that once again told her the story and that would cause her to follow him the rest of her life. He never looked at her like the sons of Korah. He always looked upon her as a person of great wealth and value. He walked slowly and deliberately as he approached her and said,

"Woman, where are your accusers? Is there anyone here to condemn you?" Mary took a deep breath for the first time in several minutes. Jesus had sent her accusers packing with their tails between their legs, and now he appeared to be setting her free from her capital offense. She drew hope. For the first time in her life here was a man that was interested in her as a human being and not as a toy for his pleasures. She quickly said, "There is none here, Lord." No one was left from the rock throwers to come and condemn this lady. You could say that Jesus pointed out the fact that they all lived in glass houses, and had no business with rocks in their hands. Instead of throwing rocks at Mary they were chased from the scene by rocks thrown in their direction and they were much more painful than the ones that would have hit Mary. The rocks that Jesus threw landed on the inside; whereas the rocks that the sons of Korah threw landed on the outside.

Moses was very limited in what he was able to do. He could only deal with the symptoms of our spiritual illness; he could not treat the source of illness. The new Moses saw the symptoms in men and wanted to deal with the source of the malady. That was his reasoning in his Sermon on the Mount, when he said, "If your right hand offends you cut it off and if your right eye causes you to stumble tear it out and throw it from you." In other words, get to the source of what is causing your hands and your eyes to sin against God. The old Moses simply cut off the hands, and asked for an eye for an eye and a tooth for a tooth. On the surface it would appear that Jesus was much harsher on the scoundrels with the roving eyeballs but actually he was saying to his followers, deal with the source of your spiritual problems. The new Moses focused his attention on the sources, the old Moses could only deal with the symptoms of the source and that he did very poorly and very crudely.

The new Moses looks at Mary who had been shaking like a leaf even though she kept up a brave front and says, *"Neither do I condemn you. Go your way and sin no more."*

Now this can be awfully confusing to a person like Mary who knew the streets and the people of the streets very well. If Jesus was telling her to never sin again then he would be in conflict with quite a few scriptures of the New Testament. So, not to sin ever again is not the issue here. The issue here is the sin of adultery. He did not want her to be in trouble again by committing adultery because this caused all sort of family fights and disruption. Besides, it was not the safest occupation in the world. People have a tendency to get fairly violent when their mates are involved with someone else. Mary walked away with her life and her new found sense of freedom. Maybe God wasn't this horrible person in the sky holding on to a huge stick waiting to clobber her. Maybe he was a little bit different than what she knew of Him.

On this day, Jesus endeared himself to the masses and his story would be the stuff legends are made of and recounted in circles all over Jerusalem. He had the authority to stone this woman seeing that he lived a perfect sinless life which gave him the right to point the finger. Yet he did not. He pulled his punches and dealt with the internal rather than what was obvious externally. His mission on earth was not judgment but reconciliation[34]. Of this he had to remind his disciples constantly; given that they wanted him to call on the fire from heaven to come down on everybody that didn't agree with them or who gave them a difficult time. The sons of Korah never understood that fact or his mission. All of their lives they had been playing musical chairs with God as they circled the throne of God, looking for the first opportunity and vacancy in the Trinity. It never occurred to them that God preferred mercy over judgment.

Is it possible that God has provided a better way to be holy and live righteously before him? Living the obedient life is not working very well for the Mary Magdalene's of this life. Liars and sinners it

---

[34] John 3:17

has made of everyone, therefore there must be a better way or we will all be having dinner with the Korahites in a very hot restaurant.

Is the essence of the righteous life what Abraham found after he had committed the same sin as Mary from Magdela, or is it what Moses found when he became a murderer and killed the Egyptian soldier and was not stoned for being a murderer? Is this new righteousness what David discovered after he became a murderer and killed the Uriah the Hittite after committing adultery with his wife? Was this righteous life discovered by Paul after he jailed and killed the Christians of the first century?[35] All over Jerusalem people were drinking new wine out of new wineskins; the old wineskins were fading away and could not handle the new wine being offered. They were dressing themselves in festive new garments that required no cleansing and no patches to repair because they could not become torn, spotted, or wrinkled. The enthusiasm was spreading all over Jerusalem and building into a fever pitch. It was becoming a party, a celebration that the King was throwing for his son until the sons of Korah stepped in and put a stop to it out of jealousy, anger, and rage.

She was a lovely young lady that day that she introduced herself to me at church. Her eyes were bright beautiful and dark which complimented her slightly tanned skin tone. Attending church was a regular occurrence for her as she was an orphan and was looking for a role model to be a father figure in her life. For some reason or another she chose me to be her model not knowing how inadequate and unprepared I was and still am. I readily accepted the challenge because I am a sucker for underdogs in life and she was definitely an underdog. Life had been extremely cruel to her but she had refused to give up; as her eyes went from face to face in the congregation looking for a kind smile and a place to call home. A home with hearts full of love and unconditional acceptance had been her dream. As I began to befriend her I knew that I could not provide a home for her but that I could be a father figure at least. Then she began to ask me

---

[35] Acts 7:58-60

to do fatherly things. One day she asked me to come to her recital and to watch her play her instrument. "Will you come and please watch me play?" Now I am an athlete of the rough tuff cut. I have been the macho type all of my life and to be asked to come to a recital was the last thing that I wanted to hear but at the same time I did not want to disappoint my little fragile friend. I reluctantly said yes, just to get her off my back and hoping the issue would go away and be forgotten. I have good intentions but good intentions are not always the best things to have unless you plan to follow through. S*he was devastated!* She had spent the entire recital looking for me and I was nowhere to be found. The results of that broken promise still linger in my memory. It wasn't so much the broken promise that hurt as much as it was the look on her face, when I saw her next that wiped me out. When she found me on Sunday night at church, she had very little to say. Her eyes however, said volumes to me. Very quietly, just above a whisper, she said, "I was expecting you." I was crushed. What had started out as something that was good; ended up being something that was bad. I had good intentions but carrying out these good intentions did not happen. My good intentions were of no value to me or to anyone else. Saying, I'm sorry just did not cut it at that point seeing that my conduct was inexcusable. A promise had been broken, a trust had been shattered and so was I. This young orphan who so desperately wanted a father figure was left holding the bag once again. Another failure had come into her life another promise to her had been broken.

The drive home from church was long, very long. The sermon that the preacher gave... I could not tell you one word that was said or heard by me after the service. I went home that night as usual to an empty house and a haunting memory. I had failed to keep my promise, and my standards. My prayer to God was to ask him why was I so weak in keeping promises, standards, laws, rules, regulations. For every rule or law that I had ever raised in my life, there was a law that was broken and a broken promise. It was devastating to me and to those around me. I screamed at God in my prayers, partially being angry because of my failure with the young orphan and my inability to keep his word. Every bar that I had raised at some point I ended up crawling beneath it. The law makes a liar out of me, good intentions not kept make me a hypocrite, and to deny those facts meant that the problem is much more severe than I realized.

Why Lord? Why can't I keep your law? Why did Moses and the Hebrews break the law ten minutes after they had received it? What is it about rules, laws, standards, covenants, regulations that make us into liars and hypocrites?

The answers to these questions lie in the disciple of Jesus that had Christians killed and jailed before he became a disciple. His testimony begins as such. *"I know perfectly well what I am doing is wrong. There is no question that my actions are wrong and my thoughts are wrong, but at times I find myself powerless to stop and helpless to do anything about it. Inside of my being there is a beast that I cannot control and does not want to be controlled even by God."* God does not have a plan for his redemption as he simply must die out when the soul leaves the body. *"The beast inside of me is hideous and can be extremely cruel at times. I hate it but it is a much a part of me as eating food and drinking water every day. It is a natural part of my existence; it desires to dominate my soul and to control my very existence. Except for the grace of God, I would be a violent criminal. When I have good intentions, I don't carry them out. When I try not to do wrong, I end up doing it anyway. It seems in this life I am destined to be a spiritual failure, even though deep inside I desire very much to be pleasing to my God. Of all the people on the face of this earth, I must be the most wretched one of all. In my prayers, I scream, 'Is there anyone who can deliver me from this death from this evil that is in my very limbs and soul?'*[36]

This was the testimony of the greatest Christian who has ever lived. His name was the apostle Paul and he wrote a large portion of the New Testament. There is little comfort in knowing that the

---

[36] Romans 7 (paraphrased)

greatest apostle of all struggled with the very same things that we all do. My soul cries out for RIGHTEOUSNESS. I want to be righteous before God.

So what's a fellow to do? Where do we go? Paul screams out for the living God and listens for the answer. The Holy Spirit tells him that Jesus Christ has delivered him and is in the process of delivering him from the old evil master and beast of the soul.[37] Jesus will deliver you. Please note that it is a person who will deliver you and not the church, not an organization, not a discipline, not religion, not positive thinking. It is a person who delivers from the broken promises, laws, rules, and regulations. It is a person who has given me hope and answers not a system or an organization. This person dries my eyes at night and lifts up my head during the day and places my feet on a solid path as I walk with him. He bears the load of guilt and shame that my old evil master loves to dump on me on a daily basis.

You may ask the question of why are things so different now than they were before. It is because I am involved in a relationship. I am not keeping rules, laws, and regulations. This has been tried and found lacking. Now I desire to keep my promises to the orphans that looked to me for help and guidance. Now I am empowered to keep the promises and the old evil master has been nullified.

Moses broke his promises, covenants, and laws as soon as he came down from the mountain and found the Hebrews in the midst of an immoral and wild party. His fits of uncontrollable rage and anger got him in trouble and cost him a trip into the promise land. The Hebrews broke the laws of God when Moses came down from the mountain and found them in the midst of an orgy. Is it possible for us to keep God's law and be righteous and holy before him when the greatest men of the bible failed and could not keep the laws, promises, and commands of God? Pause friend when you think of Abraham's adultery with Hagar. Think about Moses who was suppose to have been stoned to death as a murderer himself. Does

---

[37] Romans 3:10-18

David give you a reason to think when you realized that he murdered the man after he had committed adultery with his wife?

The reason why a relationship with God becomes so much more effective when you're not merely trying to be obedient to him; is because the relationship effectively removes the law from becoming a factor; because as soon as the law becomes a factor so does sin[38]. After the fall of Adam I had to conclude that Jesus does not expect anything of me but failure in the spiritual life in all aspects. But the moment that he becomes a factor in my spiritual life, things change. When I add Jesus to my failure the outcome is now different. Now my relationship is not based on fear, and trying to live a holy and righteous life; it is based upon Christ in me; the hope of glory. I keep God's word because there is a desire in my heart to do so; based on a loving and understanding relationship and not on one of fear, guilt, condemnation, and hell fire and brimstone preaching. Where there is no law, there is no condemnation.[39]

I like the new wine that Jesus has given me to drink. I like the new garments that he has given me to wear. I love the new shoes that fit my feet perfectly for walking with him every day. My ears which were full of wax have been cleaned so that I can hear the Holy Spirit speaking to me day after day. The path that I once walked has been redirected from misery and destruction to a new path that is pointing the way to the celestial city and the promise land.

What the New Moses did for Mary Magdalene who was judged so harshly by the sons of Korah, he has done for everyone because it is not only Mary who was caught in adultery, it is also you and I. The woman from Magdela became a faithful disciple of Jesus Christ. After he freed her from the trap that had been set by the sons of Korah, she was free to make a decision to follow him or free to go home and to resume her life. She chose to follow the man from Galilee. The new Moses who had delivered her out of her Egypt of sin had to power to do what the old Moses could not do.

---

[38] Romans 7:13
[39] Romans 8:1-4

The new Moses gave her the new covenant that he brought down from the mount of Beatitudes with him after 40 days of fasting. This new covenant was unconditional and could be kept only by him or broken only by him. The new covenant that he made with her was to put his laws in her heart and not on tablets of stone to be broken again. This of course is a reference to the Holy Spirit.[40] God spoke through Jeremiah after the failure of laws and covenants that he would write his laws upon their hearts and he would be their God and they would be his people. Jesus gave Mary a new nature to follow so that she would not be dominated by the beastly nature in her. Along with the new nature he gave her forgiveness of sins and a secure future with himself. He gave her the righteous life. The will of God was no longer burdensome to her because she delighted to do the will of God. She had the power to keep her promises to others in Christ Jesus because all of the requirements and promises of the law and the scriptures had been met through Jesus Christ who now lived in her. Mary was free to concentrate on her new found relationship with Christ as opposed to crawling beneath the laws and statutes placed upon her. The Christian life for her had already been lived and the victory over sin and death had already been won. She was now walking in that victory and living in that life just as Abraham her forefather did when the Lord told him to walk before him and be righteous.

Today, the little orphan girl that I befriended in Arkansas hopefully has a home and a family of her own. I pray that the memories of my failure to live up to the father figure that she wanted and needed have been erased. They have not been erased from my memory. Oh...if we could only start all over again and do things differently. I pray that she has a husband who loves her dearly and that she is able to look up to him and to admire him. I pray and hope that she has put her trust in the living God who will not fail her as I did.

---

[40] Romans 8:1-4, Jeremiah 31

Not long before his crucifixion the old Moses found himself in the land of Canaan of all places.[41] Can you believe it? Isn't God a good God? Isn't God an awfully gracious God? The old Moses finally did make it to the land flowing with milk and honey but it was only by the grace of God. His disqualification had been taken away. The curse had been reversed. And now the old Moses was living in the land that he saw from Mount Nebo and could not enter. The land that he had prayed and petitioned God to enter but God had absolutely refused to allow him to go in. He was there. Yet, as far as the sons of Korah were concerned it was entirely a different proposition. There may have been other arrangements made for the sons of Korah.

When the new Moses died on a mountain such as the old one did, likewise his body was not found. He indeed was the fulfillment of the prophecy of the Moses at Mt Sinai but like his predecessor he too had failed to take the Hebrew nation into the promised rest that he had told Joshua to expect. The Hebrew's were in the promise land but they were not enjoying the promises of Abraham, Isaac, and Jacob. Nor did they enjoy the rest that God had given to them. Therefore, there remained a rest for the people of God.

---

[41] Matthew 17:3

Chapter Ten

BIRTH, BAPTISM, AND THE RIGHTEOUS LIFE

It was the first of April in 1953; early on a Wednesday morning, that a frightened young mother to be by the name of Lois had made the trip up from Mulberry in a beat up old 52 Chevy pickup and walked into Risser Clinic.

The clock on the wall struck two while at the same time a loud smack on a newborns bottom was heard across the clinic; the kid from Mulberry had just arrived on the planet. From the slap on his rear end, he was not exactly in the best of moods when he took his first breath of fresh air. He couldn't decide whether to be angry at the doctor for his rudeness or to be angry at the world for having been taken out of his warm comfortable cocoon into such a hostile and cold hell on earth. It was the former that he decided to immediately take to task.

A kindly old gentleman by the name of Risser stood about 6'4" tall, weighing in at 300 pounds, with a constant red nose was the attending physician at my birth; and at this time I made sure that the clinic was not the quietest place on earth, due to my untimely entry. I don't remember if my mother decided if this thing should be over very quickly after nine months, or I just got tired of being in the fetal position for nine months. Nevertheless, when I came out, I came out butt first and things haven't been the same since then. Now Dr Risser decided to bring me the world by holding me by the feet as his huge hands made sure that the air on one end came out at the other. It was as if he was saying with his slap, "Why didn't you come out the normal way that all other babies do when they are born." Well, I let him know straight up that I was not overly excited with his methods and techniques in pediatrics. As a matter of fact, I gave him a pretty good piece of my mind for the next twenty minutes or so, just to let him know that he couldn't go around treating helpless two-minute-old babies like that. From that day on every time I walked into his clinic, I gave him the old evil eye and the once over. It didn't help much because he kept sticking me in the same place with pins and needles. I shook my head because I absolutely did not know what I was going to do with him and his techniques. He resolved everything with pins and needles.

The world in 1953 was so much simpler. A loaf of bread was $.16, a gallon of milk was $.94, a new car was just over $1,800, and gas was $.22 a gallon. This was the world into which I was born; but as a result of being born after midnight and butt first, I saw the world from a different perspective. My father had left me and my mother nine months ago. He had gotten out of town while the getting was good and hasn't looked back since then.

Later on when it came time for my name to be written down on official papers and the doctor asked my mother what my name was, I just about lost it when she added my absentee father's last name to mine. I complained and yelled until I finally took my mother's maiden name. The world was upside down for me at my birth so why in the world would I want to change it; so I was christened Marsh Reginal White and that is the name that I bear today. I wanted to be identified with my mother so I kept my mother's maiden name. The good folks of Mulberry do not know Marsh White, but they are fully aware of Reg, or Reggie White. Therefore the use of my country name Reggie.

The time was 66AD and the place was the city of Rome. Legend has the apostle Peter leaving the city of Rome with his bags half packed, because of a mad man by the name of Nero. A powerful hand that only he could see grabbed his shoulder as he approached the city gates and the town limits. The man dressed in white asked him where he was headed. Seeing that most of the folks who were passing by seemed to be in a bit of a hurry, Peter looked perturbed as if to say, "I'm trying to catch the first and the fastest flight out of

Rome", now would you let go of my shoulder please. The maniac in government at that time had torched the city of Rome and resorted to blaming the wrong people. On top of all that he actually had the nerve to think that people loved to hear him play his fiddle. The angel persisted and Peter finally got the message. He slowly turned back into the city to face this mad man because Jesus would be crucified once again through him. People were streaming passed him by the hundreds with babies crying, and dogs barking, in the midst of chaos and confusion they all turned into shadows that passed in the corners of his eyes for he knew exactly what he had to do.

Two massive Roman soldiers who had assisted in the slaughters of the coliseum escorted him before Nero who spoke to Peter at the top of his voice while vacillating between an evil smile and violent outbursts of temperament that made no sense to anyone who heard him at the time. It was like looking at two different men in the same person. Peter knew that he was in trouble, the kind that you do not get out of in this life.

The next day Peter found himself in a cage as he was being pulled into the Roman Coliseum by horses. A crowd that was starved for entertainment was egged on by the emperor who could not keep his eyes from twitching or his voice at a reasonable level.

"Here is the troublemaker of Rome," the twitches came more rapidly now as he looked at Peter who was brought before the emperor's box and dragged it all around for everyone to get a good look at it. Loud whistles and jeering followed him around the arena as the patrons threw whatever they could get their hands on at Peter. Peter knew that his fate was sealed but he did not know if his fate would be that of others who had gone before him in Nero's circus. He could hear the frustrated and angry roars of lions and tigers caged up beneath the coliseum. These were lions and tigers that had been starved for this very occasion; so as to leave their natural fear of humans. He struggled to keep his dignity and composure before this hostile crowd and sadistic emperor, but it was a losing battle. Fear ravages its victim and is an ever present enemy which is hard to keep at bay.

On the very next day they dragged Peter from his cell in the Mamertine prison to a hill just outside of Rome. On the way to the hill an unexplainable peace abided upon Peter as it had with all Christian martyrs before him of that time and era. For once in his life his hands did not shake under pressure and his heart did not race in the face of death and danger. He recounted the time around the campfire right outside of Jerusalem when Jesus was being put on trial for his life when he buckled under fire. It was not so at this moment in time. He was the rock that Jesus had predicted that he would be on his final day and up to his last minute. The first nail pierced his right hand it was like someone had just taken a red hot iron out of the fire and placed it on his hand. When they pierced his left had it sent him into shock and the body began to tremble uncontrollably. And just as they were about to slam the pole into the ground, he made a last minute request with what little energy and voice he had left in him. He was totally aware that the soldiers did not know what they were doing; he was aware that their understanding had been thwarted by the world and the evil one; so he requested that his crucifixion reflect the way the world saw things from a spiritual point of view. Men's lives and God's plans for their lives had been thwarted by the first Adam who gave us the wrong view of God. Their understanding of God was taken away from them and replaced with their own erroneous views of God and the world.

So in his crucifixion, he requested to be crucified upside down. He told the attending soldiers that he was not worthy to be crucified in the same way as his Lord. They granted him his last minute request; and that was how he left this world while singing songs of glory as his ship departed from the docks. He gave us a picture, and the world a portrait. It was a picture of what Adam had done to this world and a portrait of man before God. It was a picture of what Jesus Christ would have to do in order to make things right for men and righteous before God. He would have to reverse the curse and turn the picture of God right side up. Then mankind would have understanding and insight. The world view of Adam would radically be altered, and men could have peace with the God of this universe.

So what did Adam do that was so bad that a man would have to die on a cross to undo it and others were still dying as a result of it?

Well, on March the 28th of 1978, I made a commitment to God. I committed my life to Him and I had asked to be re-baptized in honor of that commitment to Jesus Christ. I wanted this commitment to stick, not like what had happened in cousin Len's pond with all the turtles snapping at me and the snakes hissing. This time it was going to be different.

Baptism would be the wedding band on my finger; it was my way of telling the entire world that I belonged to one man and to only one God and that was the Lord Jesus Christ. It was my wedding ceremony to the King of Kings and the Lord of Lords; and I very prominently still have that ring in place today. I have become identified with the one and only true God, Jesus Christ himself. The marriage license was signed on June 5th of 1978, and today I am completely identified with Him.

However, on April 1st of 1953, I was not only completely ignorant as to what had happened to me physically but I was ignorant as to what had happened to me spiritually all so early on that Wednesday morning. For not only did a physical birth take place, a spiritual birth also took place. Now the doctor on duty at that time made sure that I was completely aware of my physical birth within minutes with a whack on my back side, and every time I returned to his clinic in my early years for some reason or another, I was awfully suspicious of his right hand. There was a, "you better watch it buster", in my tone of voice every time he spoke and I had to answer. But I was completely unaware of what had happened to me spiritually. Maybe instead of giving Dr. Risser the evil eye, I should have given Adam the evil eye because when I was born, I was completely identified with Adam, the very first man.[42] I was baptized into him without my full knowledge or permission. It was one of those weddings that are arranged at birth. Adam had slipped his wedding band on my finger by default and I was happily ignorant of that fact. Well you

---

[42] Rom 5:19

can bet your bottom dollar that I was not exactly happy about being a child bride. You talk about robbing the cradle; this is it, the very first case. A decision was made for me without my permission and there was no way out of the marriage. Well, as you would have it, I was looking for my options out of this shotgun wedding, and only one person could offer me the way out of Adam's marriage. It was not unlike what you see today with many kings and rulers who have several wives with whom they keep under lock and key with no escape. They are miserable but there is no one to come and to rescue them. Adam had me under his lock and key without my permission and I had no way to escape. My only chance was to have someone who was kind enough to come in and rescue me from this oppressive dictator. It happened in May of 1978, my liberator came to my cell block, to my dark room with no windows on it and no door knob on the inside. For the first time in 25 years I was able to see the light. I was exposed to a whole new world of **_Sonlight._** A new world awaited me, a whole new world full of love and care. My eyes that saw light for the first time; because Jesus Christ had touched them and with his touch the scales were removed and I could see all things clearly. The world was not dark and gloomy as my old master had pictured it and had not allowed me to see for myself. It was full of life and color. The Son gave light and life to me through his touch, but most importantly of all, he gave me a choice to be divorced from my old slave master Adam.[43] His light felt so good upon my face that it returned the color to me and my soul.

The old Adam scowled! He did not want to relinquish his property without a fight. In his mind I still belonged to him and he definitely wanted the keys back from Jesus. The choice was up to me to decide whether I wanted freedom or whether I wanted to be under the domination of the old nature and Adam. Adam not only protested, he protested loudly that he was the best for me. There was not an ounce of goodness in him and behind evil eyes were ruthless and murderous intentions. This understanding of God was warped, and his seeking of God was severely affected in the fall. The whole

---

[43] Romans 6:1-4

human race lies before him in condemnation before Christ came. When he speaks, his lips drip with a deadly poison and there is a foul stench coming from deep inside his throat. He is an evil, cruel master that hates God and the name of Jesus Christ. There is no fear of God before his eyes and as a result he does not respect mankind as he leads them on a pathway to misery and destruction.[44]

My release from his prison was a statement by Jesus Christ that Adam is no longer in charge and my master, and that his days are numbered. As a matter of fact, because of his actions, he was placed on death row and is now awaiting his execution. In the meantime he is making phone calls from his cell in order to influence his former victims to come and break him out of prison, but it is all to no avail. For me his influence over me is still very strong whenever he speaks. At times I often forget that a condemned man is speaking as though he is my owner and master and I buy into his rhetoric. Whenever he speaks, it is always from a nature of evil and vicious lies[45] that sounds very much like the truth because I have bought into the lie for so long. Most of his lies are in the area of my spiritual life in an effort to get me to focus on something other than Jesus Christ, and he is constantly condemning my soul and demanding perfection from me. When I do not perform, this vicious hate rhetoric begins over and over again until I actually believe the lies that he told me about myself as facts. He makes me to jump through his hoops of lies and deceptions until I believe.

Adam's best weapon is the subtle lies that he tells me, and his slick method of making me believe that his thoughts are my true thoughts and feelings. He is excessively cruel, but incredibly effective. He absolutely hates God and Jesus Christ and deep down inside he is murderous and self-destructive. Who has the power to deliver me from the body of this death? Who can take the keys away from sin and death? Who has the power to put his foot upon the

---

[44] Romans 3:10-18
[45] Romans 3:13

neck of this old evil and wicked master in order to march his rotting corpse into the grave that has his marker on it?

The apostle Paul who found the answer shouted out the answer from a Roman dungeon, but I could not hear it, at the time of his shouting: my ears were clogged by my efforts to be right before God, religion, and being religious. I could not hear him or his message. My world view had not been righted as of yet. Adam was well pleased. He was deeply satisfied with my religious activities and Bible studies. It pleased him to no end when I handed out tracts and tried to live a sinless life. But he grew very concerned when I focused on Jesus Christ alone and the workings of the Holy Spirit in my life. So he kept me busy with crusades, religious activities, and camps which gave me a satisfaction that I was winning the world for Jesus Christ. He knew that he had lost the war in my life, but the battles were not over. It is not unlike the Japanese veterans who were found in the jungles long after World War II was over who were still fighting a war that was over long ago. The old Adam in me did not want to hand over his weapons of destruction voluntarily. They have to be ripped and torn out of his cold dead hands. It gives him great pleasure whenever there is a victory in my life that he has orchestrated.

One of Adam's most deadly strategies is to appear as an angel of light to make me believe that what I am doing has great spiritual value. Now that he is on the defensive, he does not like to be identified as the obvious; so he uses different covers. He likes to blend in with the crowd so as to mask his real intentions. It is when I take a serious look at my true motives that I can see his fingerprints such as tithing. Why do I give to my church? It is to really show my love for God and to build up his Kingdom or am I afraid of the devourer that many ministers use to threaten congregations. What is my true motive in giving to the church? Is it to give to God what is due to Him? Or do I just want him off my back for the rest of the week, which was the case with Cain? God does not enjoy that kind of giving any more than I do. It is at these times when I ask the hard questions that I can see the fingerprints of Adam. There are hard questions that deal with the spirit of the law; which Adam does not like; because it forces him out of his kingdom of darkness and legalism, and into God's marvelous light. He does not like the truth of God if it is not to his advantage or if it can't be manipulated in a way so as to bring people under his rule once again. The darkness and the night are his nature and sweetness to his soul. Here he can destroy the plans and efforts of his arch enemy, Jesus Christ. Good intentions, hard work, can be used with great spiritual leverage, and as a substitute for true spirituality. The Christian who wants to please God with all of his heart can easily be misled and Adam counts on it. Let him keep up his charade of good works and hard work for the Kingdom of God and it pleases him to no end. Selah. I hate the old sinful nature. I hate Adam simply because he will not allow me to reach out and get the true spiritual prize; the one for which God has called me into this race. I am always a day late and a dollar short with Adam. He is so incredibly devious to me and there is absolutely nothing that I can do to change him one iota until he is laid to rest in my coffin and my rotting corpse is beside him. His favorite muscle is his hiding muscle that he flexes to no end. It was him who had returned to my bedroom one night after I was baptized in Mulberry in Cousin Lens pasture. He never gave me one moments rest from his demands on me and my flesh; he simply made sure that they were covered up with religious fervor and zeal.

It is very much like what I use to witness in my church back home when the choir either forgot the words or could not carry or even remember the tune to the song. Cousin Kermit had this really deep bass voice that you could hear for a country mile away. His singing raised more than just dead folks from the grave, it kept the entire congregation from going to sleep. I would say that it covered up his inability to sing, but that would be a compliment. Whenever the old Adam is at his best, you can rest assured that it is a cover up. Someone is about to get gypped and it is usually the person who is wearing his skin for that day. That would be me. I have been gypped so many times that you would think that I would have learned my lesson by now. I'm a sucker for a good song and dance routine with religious fervor. My old nature is counting on it. He absolutely loves it when I go home from church feeling good but can't remember what has been said from the sermon that was just preached – which was not exactly the most difficult thing in the world to do, given some of the sermons that I have heard. After much ado about nothing the majority of us retire to our homes after a long and laborious service in order to settle in for the night with our old familiar friend and foe with a renewed determination to do much better the next Sunday. Our old human nature simply reaches over and pats us on the head and gives us a big knowing smile for he actually loves human effort and human sacrifice. Adam loves the pulpit on Sunday morning at eleven o'clock. One of his most favorite subjects, of course, is money; not necessarily his money, but your money on which he wants to get his grubby little hands for the glory of God's kingdom. On this particular Sunday in my church, he stopped his hellfire and brimstone preaching long enough to talk about the giving of my hard earned income. Of course, all the great promises come with his well rehearsed sermon saying that I would be blessed of God if I gave it and cursed if I didn't give it. Well, my mama didn't raise me to be the biggest fool on the block and it didn't take me long before I began to put two and two together. Let's see now, "*Do I want to be blessed today or cursed by God tomorrow?*" Which should it be! This is a hard one! For some reason I decided that I wanted to be blessed by God today. Don't ask me why, but I think it was the better deal. So, I forked over my 10% of my income. Now the question arises, "should I tithe on my gross income or my net income," and Adam's answer is the same. Do I want to be blessed on my gross or blessed on my net income? Silly me! How could I ask such a dumb question as that? It was so obvious and clear. So when the collection plate comes around, I very proudly put my little check in there expecting to be blessed somewhere between my gross and my net; not that it would be that much anyway. I saw my first cousin put money in the plate and take some out. Can you believe it? Man is he going to be struck dead by God. To my surprise, I was blessed indeed, but it was not from God, it was from my local bank. I received this very nice and not so formal looking envelope with very distinguished writings on the front, but on the inside was a disturbing looking pink colored

A HUDDLE FOR RIGHTEOUSNESS

slip of paper. I rushed to open my blessings and there it was; a check with all kinds of official looking stamps on the front and back asking me to send them money. This document had rubber stamped all over it. My blessings to the church had bounced and now the bank was asking for a blessing of a different sort. Well I wrote and told them that they could not get blood out of a turnip to which they replied, *"We will settle for the turnip, just get our money to us or else."* Of all the most embarrassing moments of my life, this took top billing. I had broken the law to try and keep the law. I could fit right in with the sons of Korah. They would have welcomed me as a card carrying charter member. How could I? How could I have written a hot check to pay my tithes? I wanted to run and hide from man and God. I so much wanted to win His favor and I had ended up in disfavor before God and man.

Well, I guess the next best thing for me was to expect a visit from the devourer which the preacher had mentioned over and over again. You know the one that the prophet Malachi talks about when he describes a man that has robbed God. Rev. Blanton had told me that he would come and take his dues come hell or high water, not unlike the mafia, and that he would leave a hole in my pocket. Well, I figured after the mortgage, the electric, gas and water bills, he might have to take a ticket and get in line because not only were there holes in my pocket, there was going to be holes in my underwear behind bars, if I could not pay my bills on time and pay off my hot check. As I ponder my early years in Christianity many things have been made clear.

There is absolutely no reason to put that kind of guilt trip on the people of God who love Jesus Christ dearly and desire to follow Him. It is anathema! It is not the gospel of God. Solomon compares this to the pounding rain that comes to destroy the crops and then returns soon afterwards to destroy whatever is left of the crops. It is not of God, it is not even worthy to be called sacrificial giving. David is devastated after he has been laid to waste by God after his affair with Bathsheba, as Nathan comes along with his long bony finger and sticks it right into his face and says, "You are the man." David retires to his chambers where he had feasted on the lovely form of forbidden fruit and he says to God, "Sacrifice and offerings you have not desired, or else I would give them." It was the lesson of Abraham after he was asked to sacrifice Isaac, his son. God does not want sacrifice and offering, he wants the individual in the tithes. He already owns the cattle on a thousand hills and the hills themselves.

So what in the world was I doing bouncing a check trying to pay my tithes and offerings? Adam can be incredibly devious but you can add to that; incredibly manipulative. God is so gracious and good that he sent me a counselor even one who comes alongside to assist in times of trials and struggles. And the Counselor put his hands into the tender but charred areas of my life and said to me, "Why did you allow Adam to put you under the law like that? Don't you know that we are no longer under the law but under grace?" Well that was all that I needed to hear. I found every penny that I could scrounge and went in to pay off the extortion money. On that day the chains began to drop off and new life for me began. Rev. Blanton would no longer be able to put me under his spell of law and legalism anymore, not that I particularly liked to listen to him or his sermons anyway. My grandfather never did like Rev. Blanton anyway, and now I did not like Rev. Blanton, or his bad piano playing wife with her favorite song of *"whatcha gon do when the world's on fire ya."* Rev. Blanton received his pink slip from me along with the horse on which he rode. Our chickens would be much safer for now and our Sunday afternoon dinners normal once again. I was set and poised to receive a new baptism that would negate the teachings of legalism of Adam.

Chapter Eleven

The year was 1973. It was a long hot summer as I had returned home to find that nothing much had changed since I had left home. There were the same old houses beside the same old trees that stood beside the same old dirt roads. The White clan decided to move across town, or should I say further down the dirt path, so that we could give the old place back to its original owners who were the cockroaches and their descendants a thousand times over. They were happy and we were elated. They were taking over anyway and just about to run us out of town. They were pretty fed up with our mattresses that hadn't been changed in forty-five years and had suffered through 500 wet diapers from the newborns of the house. But the really big thing that made us decide to move was when my brother crawled under the bed with a candle in his hand to see what was making the squeaking noise as it slithered across the floor; and that's when the trouble started. The house caught on fire. My brother may have been somewhat brave but he was not the sharpest knife in the kitchen. The nearest fire station was twenty-four miles away as the crow flies; and besides our only method of communication was to holler down the road to grandma's house. Telephones weren't invented until 1985. We were in a pickle! The nearest water was a small pond where we used to try to catch crawdads; (for you city folks that is Latin for crayfish). My cousin Polly Mae from the city used to come down and catch them with her bare hands; pop their tails off and eat them in the raw. What a woman! I didn't have too many role models back then, but when I saw that, she went to the top of my list. Her stock soared that day in Mulberry. It was from this creek that we scooped out enough water to put my brother's fire out. We were angry and wanted to lynch my brother, and the cockroaches were royally pissed that they would have to spend the night outside and whatever it was that was crawling and slithering beneath the bed hissed and went away. Everybody gave my brother the once over along with the long rope in the back barn. Seeing that everyone was up in arms, we decided that it was time for us to move and that we did, into a new five thousand-year-old house with the shingles falling off that was pea green in color. It may not have been the best in Mulberry but to us it was the Hilton, we were the upper middle class of the share croppers now. It had another big cast iron stove in the center of it and another cooking stove of cast iron in the kitchen. We had a well in the back of it but we still had not made the move to indoor plumbing; which still made the midnight runs in the winter with the weather in the mid teens, very interesting.

One early summer day we looked up and saw an unusual but beautiful sight coming towards our house with a long cloud of dirt rising behind it. It wasn't Cousin Kermit's loud car; it was Bubba Charlie's truck. It was the newest and brightest red Chevrolet Impala that we had ever seen. It pulled in front of our font yard as the driver did his best to put his new found idol on display right beside our old '52 Chevy pickup. It was Ruby's new boyfriend. You remember Ruby don't you? She is my aunt, the one who told me that I was going to hell on roller skates. You remember – the one who told me that puppies did not belong in bulldog conversation. Her boyfriend had come down for a visit and a year later they were married. Soon after marriage, Ruby became pregnant with her firstborn child as her husband went away to Vietnam at the time. During her stay with us, she became larger and larger but to me it never appeared that things were changing for her and her baby. All that I remember during that time is being chased out of the house with a load of rocks aimed right at the center of my head. What was the big deal with Ruby? Why was she so upset and angry with me all of a sudden? Finally my grandfather spoke up and said, "Boy, you just don't understand do you?" What was there to understand? Ruby was Ruby, just because she had gained a few pounds, I didn't see any difference. All that I knew now was that the rocks and stones were coming a lot faster and harder and I was thoroughly enjoying paying her back for sending me to hell. What I truly did not understand was that a new life was

A HUDDLE FOR RIGHTEOUSNESS

coming into the world. A baby was about to be born and I knew very little about the circumstances surrounding it and the new birth.

The time was around 30AD in the city of Jerusalem in the nation of Israel. There was a man of letters among the Pharisees who sought Jesus out by night. He was not as harsh a critic of Jesus as were the others because the Spirit of the living God had an opening into a heart that was once shut and closed. He had been into many debates with the sons of Korah over this man and who he was and what he represented and no headway was made on either side. But inside of him a light was beginning to shine and the more he asked questions, the brighter the light burned in his heart. Jesus was camped out with his disciples outside of the city of Jerusalem, when they heard a rustle in the leaves, Peter, of course, was the very first to grab his sword and to investigate the disturbance. Jesus very gently asked his impulsive friend to put away his sword, and that is when Nicodemus popped out from behind the trees there in their campsite on the hillside. Jesus got up and started towards him; he looked past his eyes and into the very soul of Nicodemus. He knew why he had come. He knew instantly that the Holy Spirit had sent the man directly to see Him. Nicodemus, for fear of losing his position, had made sure that he was alone and reassured the disciples that no one had followed him. His mind was burdened; burdened and pregnant with a thousand questions that he needed to ask Jesus Christ. He knew too much. He knew too much because of what Isaiah had taught him and the Psalmist had sung to him; and not only that but he had seen too much. This man standing before him and peering into his soul could do things that no other human being could do. He had powers to heal of which the doctors of that day were useless. He had power over nature whereas he could walk on water and he could turn that same water into wine. But the most impressive thing of all was the power over the human soul. He could forgive sins. That seemed to be the major attraction for him and for most people was that Jesus had forgiven them for their sins; not unlike the sons of Korah who held people's sins against them. And people could sense in Him that He had the authority to forgive them. The miracles of Jesus were signposts for people like me who according to my Aunt Ruby were going to hell in a hand basket. She did her very best to scare the hell out of me, but I think she could have been much more effective if she had told me about the miracles of Jesus because for certain she could have appealed to my rational side. I think she really liked to scare puppies. I personally think that she and Rev. Blanton had my number. The one didn't want me to talk and the other one didn't want me to listen. I was a dead duck on a barbecue grill as far as they were concerned. But it was these miracles that went directly to the psyche of Nicodemus; you could not deny them. People can say anything and get away with it but Jesus had said it and proved with His life and His deeds. So this old Pharisee began putting two and two together; what the scriptures had said and what Jesus was doing. Jesus offered objective proof of what He was and who He is by the miracles that He did. So that now for Nicodemus everything boiled down to a matter of choice. Would he believe his very own eyes or would he listen to the rhetoric of the sons of Korah whose morality was now dictating their theology? And this indeed was a deadly game of chicken for the scribes and Pharisees of that day. They had deliberately chosen to ignore the miracles of Jesus calling him a magician and a sorcerer of that day. To them what He did was nothing more than a cheap trick which was performed in much the same way as Jannes and Jambres did when they faced Moses in the courts of Pharaoh. But Nicodemus saw more than a cheap trick. It is hard to trick people into getting up out of a grave when they have been placed six feet under. So this was why Nicodemus was puzzled. This Jesus had the ability to give life to a dead man and for all practical purposes Nicodemus was a dead-man-walking who, in a few years, would find a hole in the ground as a permanent residence.

    The two men stood face to face and Nicodemus said, "Master, we know that you have been sent from God for no one can do what you do unless God is with him." He had the same look of confusion in his eyes that I did when my grandfather told me to stop harassing my Aunt Ruby who was nine months pregnant and about to give birth while at the same time preparing to take a life; namely mine.

A HUDDLE FOR RIGHTEOUSNESS

As new life was about to come forth in Mulberry so it was much the same for Nicodemus; the Holy Spirit of the living God was about to deliver a spiritual newborn into the Kingdom of God. Nicodemus was in the process of being born again. His face revealed the agitation and stress of a young mother-to-be with her first child; but I have yet to know of a baby who says to his mother, "*I think that we should all stop this process*", I've had enough. No, that baby is coming whether the mother likes it or the doctor hates it. It is still coming. So it is with the new birth. Nothing has the power to stop the process. Jesus induces the labor, when He tells Nicodemus that no one can enter the Kingdom of God unless he is born again. Well, that just about did it. If that didn't sink the boat, nothing else could. Old Nicky and I were on the same page when it came to getting into the Kingdom of God. He was looking forward to a throne in heaven and a crown on his head because of his service; his good works, tithing, his giving to the poor, but most of all because he was Jewish and a son of Abraham. This was his guarantee and eternal non refundable warranty. Jesus had just pulled the plug on him and his theology. Nicodemus, like me and my tithing every Sunday and Wednesday, was a card carrying member of the Legalism and Law Lodge. We know all the signs and passwords as charter members, and we voraciously try to recruit others into becoming members of our lodge. We give away free vacations and airline miles as long as you are legalistic and judgmental. Jesus was just too liberal for us; he would have been kicked out as he was just the opposite in the manner he treated people. He wasn't hard enough on them. He never made people feel guilty enough and he certainly never condemned them. He never would have made it into our club. And what is the deal with this born again stuff; can a man go back into his mother's womb and be born all over again?

New births are complicated! The birth process itself is complicated and miraculous. When my other brother was born, the one who did not set our house on fire, I was told by my mother to stay at home while they went down to grandma's house. It was a very long wait for me of several hours in the little wooden house all alone. I had plenty of time to think and to wonder what all the excitement was about. I was nervous because whenever there was silence in the household, it usually was not very good news. Later on, at about one in the morning, my mother and grandmother returned after I had sat on the edge of the bed staring straight ahead for hours at a time. My mind was pregnant with a thousand questions that I wanted to ask everyone, but the people of my day did not openly talk about sex and having babies. There was plenty of evidence that it was happening a lot, it was just that no one was allowed to talk about it or to explain it to the young people. There were plenty of babies around but I was supposed to believe in the stork. So I got all my information from my peers about how people became pregnant. The range of ideas was quite extensive from a bar of soap to drinking some white lightning. Being the philosopher of my house, I chose something in between the two. When everyone had finally settled into the candlelit house that night and the excitement was over, my mother called me over to come and look at my new baby brother. I remember thinking where in the world did he come from and why was he here. This is so miraculous and mysterious.

Jesus' reply to Nicodemus' question of being born again was for him to consider the wind; because you do not know from whence it came and to where it is going, but you know that it is there. You can see its effect and feel it on your face. So, it is with everyone who is born of the Spirit.

The salvation that God gives to us was nowhere close to what I experienced in my church in my home town with the pastor's wife jumping the pew and rolling on the floor and screaming to the top of her voice in order to get my cousin Len to join the church and get saved. But brother it sure made an impression on me at the time. As I take a harder look at the words of Jesus, I see a different picture today and I can understand the confusion of the Nicodemus's. The salvation process is much like the wind with no one knowing exactly where it starts or where it's going. It is totally under the control of God who sends it to and from his heaven as he sees fit and chooses.[46]

---

[46] John 1:12-13

Now, I am the seed of my father! There are no ifs and or buts about it. I am his seed for good or evil. The union with my mother came in the summer of '52 as far as I can tell and then we were left all alone to make it on our own. If my father were to stand in front of me at this moment, I would not know him or even recognize him. During my lifetime there have been no attempts for contact with either me or my mother and no complaints. This is the station that God has given to me in my life and I fully accept it. What began in my mother's womb is now entering the aging process from having been born of corruptible seed. I guess you could say that it started back with his father and his father's father, going all the way back to Adam. God told Adam, after the fall of dying spiritually, he would surely die a physical death and I and my father and the recipients of this corruptible seed. I will die and go the way of all the earth and so will all the creatures of this earth. My father's name is Naaman; and not knowing very much about him, I can see from my own personal life that what I inherited from him was both the good and the evil. My mother and I have never sat down and discussed these issues at length and I have decided not to force the matter. Many times, in prayer, I have asked God why he allowed me to grow up in a fatherless home with a grandfather that I called Daddy instead of my real father. And as always, his answers were very clear and very reassuring to me in which I take great comfort to this day.

If my real father only knew the damage and the void that were inflicted by my growing up in a fatherless home maybe things would have been different. But, for some reason or another I do not think that it would make one bit of difference to him. In many fatherless homes the well is empty when it comes to relationships. My view of God, which is supposed to come from my father, has been slightly skewed. That is why when I would be on my back in the long green grass outside of my house and talk to my friend Ronnie about God, I knew very little about him. I knew that he was far away and distant and possibly angry at me for my sins, but never saw him as being up close and personal and loving me unconditionally. My earthly father was distant and unknowable so why shouldn't my God be distant and unknowable. This corruptible seed of which I was born has not only brought all sorts of spiritual ills but indeed social ills upon me as well; mainly the problems of dealing with authority figures. I figured as far as authority figures go, if I have been living my life on my own, why should I allow for anyone to interfere now. But God is so good to the fatherless and the widows that often times he has other plans in mind, whether I like it or not.

After growing up into a full fledged adult, God began to get my attention gradually. It began with the preaching of His Word through a man out of California by the name of Chuck Smith. I loved his style of preaching and teaching as I would listen to him over and over again on the radio, and the Spirit of the living God used the word of God to plant a seed within me and I began to grow spiritually. And today after many years of germination of the seed inside of me, I was born again to a new birth by the Spirit of God. Yes, today I have joined the ranks of the Nicodemus's who have had the seed planted in them and watched it blossom into new life. Yes, I am the spiritual seed of my Father in Heaven. The apostle Paul makes reference to this in his letter to the Corinthians when he said, "I planted, Apollo's watered, but it was God who gave the increase."[47] Now to tell you the truth, if Rev. Blanton planted anything in my heart, I don't know exactly what it was; but this I do know, I am still taking medicine for it. Nevertheless, the seed of the Lord was planted and it is growing today even as I write to you beloved. The apostle Peter says that the seed that was planted inside of me as incorruptible, eternal, and fades not away.[48] With this incorruptible seed comes a new divine nature[49] which was granted to us as part of his most precious and magnificent promise. This new Father did not leave me as my old father did because He sent His Holy Spirit to reside in my heart. He has given not only to me great and precious promises, but to all of us. It is with this new nature that I have the righteous life imputed to me[50] at my salvation. It is the gift of God at the moment of my

---

[47] 1Corinthians 3:6
[48] 1Peter 1:18-25
[49] 1Peter 1:4
[50] Romans 4:6,22

salvation and a down payment of what is to come. For the first time in my life I had a Father who loved me and cared for me and had left me an inheritance; his righteousness. My new Father was not only taking care of me at the moment of my conception and birth, he was also taking care of me for all eternity by giving me the inheritance of a righteous life.[51] I knew what I was going to do when the world was on "fire ya" Sis. Blanton. And I know now, why God allowed me to grow up in a fatherless home for the very simple reason that He and He alone wanted to be my Father without the interference of my old father Naaman. Not only do I have a new Father, but I also have a new identity, a new name, and a new master. There is a new sheriff in Mulberry, Texas, and in the life of the kid from Mulberry, Texas. He did not become the new sheriff by the democratic process but rather through the deeds that he did to earn his new office.

It began right after a hairy skin man dressed in camel's hair baptized him in the Jordan River, and then a voice was heard to say this is my beloved Son with whom I am well pleased. The camel-haired man looked as Jesus left the river and said to his audience, "Behold the Lamb of God who takes away the sins of the world." It is here that Jesus sat his jaw to undo what the first Adam did to the entire human race. As he faced the mountain in the wilderness, he knew that his would be the first of many showdowns with his old enemy Satan. Personally I don't think Satan was overly excited about this showdown coming up. He knew that he was just about to get three black eyes, one for each eye and another for the road. His assassination attempts on the life of Christ had flopped in Bethlehem when he incited Herod to kill all the babies under a certain age in an effort to keep Jesus from taking over his throne. Schizophrenic kings and leaders will have a tendency to do things like that to hold onto power. He knew that Jesus couldn't be bumped off in the traditional way, so he resorted to using the same M.O. that he had in the garden with Adam. It was his only chance. His kingdom was about to be invaded by a new king and he was giving Jesus the evil eye all the way up the mountain. For forty days and forty nights they went at it,

---

[51] Romans 5:16-21

until finally he seized a great opportunity being the thief that he is. Jesus becomes hungry; it happens after 40 days of fasting. So, what do you want when you become hungry? Food! Now basically this is where Adam blew it, but the new Adam was successful. You see, Jesus was not only led by the Holy Spirit, he was empowered by the Holy Spirit. This is the model for the Christian life. This temptation went over like a lead balloon. Strike one with two left and the clock was ticking. Satan offered him money and power but all to no avail. Strike two with one left and the clock is making its rounds much faster. Now if I were one of the demons under his control, I would have demanded a new leader because this guy was getting his head bashed in just like the prophecy predicted in the book of Genesis chapter three. The last strike came when he told him to jump off the temple and then he had the nerve to quote Psalm 91 to back up what he said. Now Satan knew that it wasn't the jump that would have killed Jesus; but it was the sudden impact after the jump that God was not involved in, nor would the angels have protected him as he quoted from Psalm 91; 11,12. The quotation of the psalmist was correct, but it was the application of the psalm that would have killed Jesus. Satan lets out a big sigh as he happily leaves for fresher meat. Now this does not exactly sit well with his generals and captains who were in charge of millions of other demons. They had just been dealt a severe blow, so much so that they did not want Jesus to die on the cross, because it would be the end.

Sure enough, when Jesus was resurrected, all authority in heaven and earth was given to him[52] and as He ascended into heaven, behind Him was a long line of captives that He had conquered during his time on earth. On His ascension, He did what the original Adam had failed to do and that was to place His righteous representative into every corner of the earth. He gave them as gifts to men.[53] This was His original intention for Adam but he was not able to pull it off. The new Adam was a conqueror of men and demons and was now man's representative before God. Yes, I, too, am in that train that

---

[52] Matthew 28:16-20
[53] Ephesians 4:8

A HUDDLE FOR RIGHTEOUSNESS

He took captive but not as a slave, but as a conqueror through Jesus Christ. When He died on the cross, I identified myself completely with Him. I was baptized into His death, burial, resurrection, and ascension; and this gives me complete identity with Jesus Christ.[54] When Jesus coughs now, I catch cold. We have been joined through baptism.

Now every once in a while God tells the simple folks of Mulberry that there is a time for war and a time for peace, a time for laughter and a time for mourning. Death pounds on our door and we are none too happy to see him. We go through the usual period of mourning until the preacher preaches at the funeral; then the funeral almost turns into a riot. When a dear relative of mine died recently, we went through the funeral dirges and all was well until Rev. Blanton began to meddle and opened his big mouth (which is awfully big, by the way). He decided to lecture us in how to get along with one another. He told us with a sharp eye looking in my direction that we were not going to make it into heaven unless we all got along and learned to forgive one another. I looked at him to make sure that I wasn't listening to my Aunt Ruby all over again. I had just gotten over her sending me to hell and now he was about to start in on me, too. Wasn't this the same method of application of scripture that Satan has used on Jesus? I don't think so. It was bad interpretation and even worse application. This was awful and I wasn't about to take this any more. I had had enough of the old Adam and his yoke of bondage. It was time for the new Adam to show up. So we stepped outside and went toe to toe, nose to nose. But Rev. Blanton had to go because according to him our righteousness was based on our relationship to other people. I told him this was a lie straight out of the pits of hell as the casket and pallbearers were eyeballing me. "Prove it," he shouted with spit flying in my face. "You'd better get right with your fellow man before you die or you are going straight to hell." Now where in the world had I heard that line before? The spitballs were flying from mouth to eyes and Lord knows where else. But I was determined that the old Adam had to go and the son

---

[54] Romans 6:1-4

of Hagar had to be cast out once again. I began to open the scriptures as Jesus did on the road to Emmaus. (*It was a lovely funeral with beautiful flowers by the way.*) I explained to him how the Hebrews in wilderness were baptized (completely identified) into Moses and how God had hitched their wagon to his fate. What happened to Moses also happened to them. I proceeded to explain to him how as Christians we have been baptized[55] into the new Moses and we are completely identified with him. Whatever happens to the new Moses happens to us; this includes his righteous life that has been imputed to us by faith.[56] From this point we went from the frying pan into the fire as the undertaker was taking measurements on the both of us with a smile on his face. Relatives scattered for cover as we went at it over and over. I was not about to give in one inch to this false prophet and besides I wanted reimbursement for all of the chickens he had eaten at my house. I made sure that he went away with three black eyes because this lie and unbiblical teaching has to be confronted and stopped.

Well, as we proceeded to the burial site, I was pretty much given the cold shoulder because in some communities, the preacher is always right even if he is wrong. Rev. Blanton gave his final eulogy with a large stick suspiciously close to his feet, and the color of red in his eyes. I remember thinking to myself, even though I gave him biblical proof of my position and very clear answers; I had won the battle, but lost the war. This was hard for me to swallow. The preachers and the people in mourning could care less if I was right; I had done it with the wrong spirit.

Then the words of the psalmist rang in my ears loud and as clear as a bell when he sang to the congregation of his day, "An ear the Lord has dug for me so that I can hear and obey." This ear is not the piece hanging on the side of your head that has a canal to the eardrum, this ear runs from the mouth of the Holy Spirit directly to my conscience and it had to be dug out. There is considerable debris

---

[55] Romans 6:1-4
[56] Romans 4:22-25

in my ears. It had been clogged by legalism, law, and the old Adam, but now the canal has being cleared and the debris have been taken away. The incident with Rev. Blanton taught me that I must have an ear to hear what the Spirit says. My theology on being right before God as a matter of imputation was right, but how in the world could I tell this to a people who needed to know. This one thing I do know today and that is that it won't be done by yelling at preachers or anyone else for that matter. Soon after that incident; a young man came to me. He was confused concerning his spiritual life and being made right before God and this time the canals to my ears were open and cleared from the debris. I gave him no standards to keep, I beat him over the head with no Bible, I did not ask him to tithe his net or gross, and I stood silently as the paper boy and I watched the Spirit of the living God do his work with me once again, imparting the righteous life to another Nicodemus asking questions in the night. It was another lesson of Abraham for another son of Abraham. This is the new covenant that God had promised where he will no longer write his laws on tablets of stone but will write it on the hearts of men; and he would be our God and we would be his people.[57] What God has done to my heart now has affected my ears so that I can hear Him; it has affected my eyes so that I can see Him more clearly. Now for the first time the world is right side up and God is sitting on His throne.

---

[57] Jeremiah 31:31-34

Chapter Twelve

It happened on Ferguson road in the late afternoon as my introduction to big city life. Witches are supposed to be riding broomsticks and be dressed in long black robes with tall pointed black hats, their face decorated by a foot-long nose covered with warts. Boy did I miss this one by a country mile. She didn't ride on a broom stick – her mode of transport was a police car. She was not dressed in a black flowing robe but wore a uniform and she didn't have a face that would give her away either – she didn't display any of those telling signs on that wretched afternoon. On my trek up Ferguson road, my car was doing its very best to make it to our destination. There was a huge hole in the windshield from an accident (that was not my fault) – it matched the one at the bottom of my shoe. But if you only make $5.25 an hour; its hand to mouth – no windshield repair in this boy's budget. I had just crawled out of the roach hotel on Estacado Street and was headed for my job at the homeless shelter. She was perched behind a huge oak tree that hid her broomstick (sorry I meant: 'police car'), when she saw me coming and decided that she needed to fill her quota for that day. The car that I was driving was a four cylinder Dodge that was hitting on its last cylinder and gasping for both gas and air. It was a hand-me-down to me as a gift, from the third generation. This car had already left me stranded in the middle of the Nowhere, Oklahoma on our maiden voyage home, with a blown transmission; so this current state of affairs was nothing new to me. If I was lucky enough to get it started, then I could stick a leg through the floorboard and push start myself. But the witch was on me…her radar had locked onto a victim as she had swooped down from her lofty position behind the tree. She closed up behind me, turned on her lights to pull me over. She asked me not to get out of the car because she was scared enough as it was; and deservedly so. I was really steaming at this point not only from the effort it took to drive this car but from the added stress her unwarranted presence imposed upon me. She then began to lecture me (as if I needed it) on the rules of wearing seat belts and having car insurance as if she was really concerned with my safety. I yelled out, "I make $5 an hour." It was a combination of anger and frustration that poverty triggers in its victims and the knowledge that no matter how hard I tried to do better in this society; I was not going to make it. Angry was not the word to describe how I felt at that moment. I was livid and she knew it. It is in moments like these that human life loses its value because you are frustrated to the point of wanting to strike out. How can you pull yourself by the bootstraps if the bootstraps are continually being cut? Life has a vice grip on your neck and it is not about to let you go. So, why not end it all with a police bullet through the brain. She had struck me down and as fast as she had come up as quickly had she gone on her way – not having a clue what she had done to me. The fine was strong and hefty; it totaled over $500. I was not speeding, nor was I driving recklessly or running a red light or a stop sign, yet I had to pay a fine of over $500 because of wearing no seat belts and having no insurance. She had a right to be afraid of me because the next step would have been to throw me in jail for attacking an officer. I was seething with rage! My fine had little to do with me hurting someone else or being a danger to society, yet it had everything to do with my being poor and homeless. My love of policemen grew exponentially that day although I knew I was wrong to think of these men and women in that way. Some were simply trying to do the very best job they could, but there were some who had points to make and they wanted to take it out on the poor and dispossessed. This officer had every right to do what she did because it was the law of the land, and I had every right to be angry with her because I was too poor to keep the laws of the land.

One of the men in my shelter who had been abused time and time again by officers of the law; when he had been stopped for the last time, he had wrestled the policeman to the ground, had taken his gun and had fired a series of angry bullets into the body of the officer who had been pleading for his life.

It is at times like these that no one wins – there are no heroes or villains. There is no justice or injustice; there are just dead bodies and grieving families left behind. There is a blind rage directed at a system that does not work and dehumanizes many of us who are truants of society. Did the officer know that I was struggling to keep a roof over my head? Did she care that I had been turned down ten thousand times during job interviews wearing the only suit that was in my closet? Did she understand that at the end of the month my friend who worked at a convenience store had to bring over canned food because my cupboard was bare? Did she know that I would have gladly repaired my car and kept it in good shape if I had the resources? None of these facts mattered to her because she was fulfilling a duty whether it destroyed a life or saved a life.

As you can tell by now, those who enforce the laws will have a long way to go before they are able to win my respect again. I had to beg, borrow, and steal in order to pay my ticket. Well, I guess it is all part-and-parcel of living in the big city; although if it were not for the law, there would surely be anarchy. There needs to be a way for the laws to be enforced against those who are lawless.

My court appearance happened that summer in the late 90's. I waited in the court room for a judge who showed up late but had the nerve to issue warrants to those who did likewise. I remember thinking; *if you are going to enforce the law on those of us who have broken the law, shouldn't you at least be innocent of breaking the law yourself or, does that really matter when you are in the position to be oppressive? Doesn't that make you some kind of a hypocrite?*

At my court appearance, there was a bad bailiff with an even worse attitude. It dripped down from his face onto his shoulders and he wore it like an award for excellence in duty. It was his court responsibility to be mean and nasty to the truants so as to help keep us in line. I very politely handed him my papers and he snatched them from my hands. It was another form of humiliation. One thought kept popping up in my mind as we sized each other up for combat, *if I ever catch you in my neck of the woods, we would have a very long and productive conversation of which you will come out on the short end of it.* He was rude to the point of being obnoxious as he turned up his nose at the poor and destitute that had to walk pass him on their way to be judged. He loved being in the judgment seat; he absolutely loved to look down his nose at people's position; he wiggled around in it and enjoyed it to the max. From that day on he became my very favorite bailiff of all times. I gave him, "Bailiff of the year," award for ten years running. When I finally made my way to the judgment bench I noticed something extraordinary! Lo and behold the city had a prosecutor – can you believe that? A prosecutor for a traffic fine; for a non-moving violation, I had to be *prosecuted*. I looked around for my court appointed lawyer to even things out and there was none to be found. Nowhere! I was alone! Thus I was bound to face judgment all alone. The judge looked at the prosecutor who brought the case against me in a most eager fashion. She exacted her every word, waved her arms, used the best of courtroom language and proved me guilty beyond any (and all) reasonable doubt! When I came into court that day for my judgment, I had no idea that I was a lamb being led to the slaughter; not a perfect or spotted lamb mind you but a lamb nevertheless that was headed for slaughter.

She was well dressed in an Armani suit fit for the day of killing lambs. You could tell that she was fresh out of law school and loved the power she obviously had to putting people away behind bars. She relished every minute of her assignment. The wicked witch of the East that had pulled me over in the police car had an evil sister, "the wicked witch of the West," and here she was in court against me. They had it in for me. I had pleaded 'no contest' and yet she presented her case before the judge with pride and gall. She was lovely but inexperienced. You know the kind. They know just enough to do more harm than good. She never looked at her victims; she refused to acknowledge their state or condition; it was irrelevant. I had broken the law and was as guilty of sin and I deserved punishment to the fullest extent of the law. You could see from the look on her face that her conscience had long been gutted from law school and lies but not from reality that had been lived out of a hard life. Her Armani suits had been charged to the number of prosecuted people

A HUDDLE FOR RIGHTEOUSNESS

of no means that had been trodden by her expensive high heeled shoes. She was on the take again and I was her victim today.

She pointed out my violations to the court and to the judge with an air of confidence and pride in her duty. I could not deny one single charge. They were all true. She had a slam dunk case against me and it was acknowledged by the fact that she rarely looked at her opponent. Her mind was on the expensive suits that she was going to purchase not on the damages being done to human life. It was a destructive power which she seemed to brandish at will and to enjoy doing so to the fullest. It had destroyed her way of thinking and now it was a virus that infected many others with whom she came into contact. It was the same power that destroyed the one who was her predecessor. She was satanically proud and happy that day for doing her part in cleaning up the big city – from *criminals* like me. This wicked witch of the West won best witch award for ten years running.

The judge was given no choice but to find me guilty as she gave me the same look that I had from the wicked witch of the East. My return glare was from a man who's used to being strapped and continually cut down. I walked out of court that day being found guilty, $500 poorer and with and even poorer view of our justice system realizing that those laws together with the system of laws were not just and did not work. *Yet, could it be that this justice system works so well that only the poor and disenfranchised show up? Wow! What a really neat system!*

All of my life I had been told stories about witches who were women with a nasty sense of humor. Three months after being molested by the wicked witch of the East her brother pulled me over for another non-moving violation. It made me so happy that people loved and cared about me the way they did in this big city! As I was watching him in my rear view mirror, I saw him nearly run over innocent people in order to get to me so that he could give me a ticket. I said absolutely nothing as I handed over my driver's license to this officer.

His reply was, "The reason that I have to give you a ticket is because I have to ticket ten people today, and you are number eight."

That really made his case. I was sitting in a new car – the other one I had given away and this one, which I bought from a fellow student, was in a better condition. It was 'rustic red' that had been bleached off by the sun, the motor was caked with years and years of dirt and motor oil, the fenders were eaten away by the salt and wear from the highway, and I was still making $5.25 an hour! I had reached my limits with policemen. If I were a criminal, I could see this harassment; if I had sold drugs, or harmed someone, I could understand getting another ticket. But it appeared that all that I needed to do was just to be a living human being and this life had decided to kick me in the teeth repeatedly. My fists were clenched and my temper was raging; to hell with the consequences. I wasn't going to be a victim anymore; nor was I going to be picked on anymore and if I were going down at least I was going to be swinging when they put the last bullet in my head.

God usually intervenes when I am in a fix like this. If this officer was going to lecture me like the wicked witch of the East did, it was going to be between knuckle sandwiches. He quickly sensed something was up and left the scene, and I was left with another court appearance. However, this time it was different. I was not going to face that wonderful bailiff and the righteous judge alone. I had to find me an advocate, a lawyer who would plead my case the way the rich people did. So, I searched for the best attorney that I could find; one that knew the system and the judge.

Unexpectedly, I stumbled across such an attorney – we discussed my case and my upcoming court appearance. He spoke in relaxing tones as if we were old friends passing the time of day. He proceeded to ask me about the court and the time of my judgment to come and in doing so he comforted me with the fact that my situation was not one that he could not handle or with which he was unfamiliar. For the first time in my life I did not feel like a victim in this life. I felt, for once, as if I had been empowered and that the boots of adversity had been lifted from the back of my neck. As a result, I actually

A HUDDLE FOR RIGHTEOUSNESS

looked forward to my day in court knowing that someone would be representing me. The person who was my representative had no records against him, no penalties to pay, and as a result was in good standing before the courts of this city.

Finally my day in court came one fall day early in the morning. This time it was going to be much different. There was calmness about me and a peace of mind. There was the absence of fear and no feelings of condemnation and sin. I was not looked upon as some criminal that was anti-social and had to be locked away. It was wonderful knowing that I had someone to stand in my stead and to deal with whom ever was again dressed in an Armani suit. For once, I was clothed in something more than fear and shame when I went before the judge. That day my attorney went toe to toe with Miss Armani. He fully explained to her that I had been legally absolved from paying any debts and penalties that the courts had against me because he had erased them all from the records; and therefore she had no basis for condemning me. With this she slithered back into the hole from whence she came in order to lick her wounds. My attorney faced the judge and he whispered something into her ear and in an instant it was over – the case against me was dismissed. Having a representative before the judge made all the difference in the world especially *if you are guilty as sin.*

As I strolled passed my friend the bailiff who, by the way, was giving me the stare down, my tongue accidentally slipped out. I don't know why, it happens on various occasions, I quickly pulled it back in, of course, as he began to share with me some things that I can't put down in this book. I was no longer the victim, and I had no need to be the victim. My foot was on the neck of the prosecuting attorney and the bailiff and it felt good.

As I walked out of the courthouse, my mind reflected on the incident with the officer; how he had come so close to destroying a life that I had dedicated to Jesus Christ. Why? Why was I so angry at this law enforcement officer who was simply trying to do his job, though he looked like he was thoroughly enjoying it? As I ponder, I realized that my anger was not so much directed against the officer as it was towards the injuries he was trying to inflict upon me with complete disregard for the consequences. The police had already taken every dime I had in the bank, and as a result my landlord had given me a month to move out. So they had taken my home and were forcing me to live on the streets and apparently it wasn't sufficient; they wanted more. I could handle my bank account being overdrawn, and being kicked out of my house, but when they wanted what little dignity I had left, I drew the line. Hell would freeze over first. That is why I know my God to be such a gracious God who delivers me whole from my enemies.

Chapter Thirteen

When God spoke to my heart in Ur of the Chaldees which is the Mulberry of my eye, I responded much like Abraham did in my belief in him and in my walk of faith. When he delivered me through the Red Sea out of the spiritual death of Egypt, I knew that he would be my God; and when he delivered me from the legalistic religion and religious systems of my day, I became his disciple and remain so even to this very day. Yes, he has put Humpty-Dumpty back together again. Jesus Christ has done what all the king's men and all the king's horses could not do. He came to my wall; he died for my fall; he has saved me from my sin; and through his death, burial, and resurrection, he has put me back together again. He put together what the Rev. Blanton's of this world had shattered and had thrown out with last night's trash.

The Mosaic and Pharisaic systems today are prevalent throughout the land. They still cling to the old vine and to the old wineskins that were shattered when Jesus Christ was resurrected. Today they still carry around shadows and types of yesteryear when they could have the substance of their shadows which has been raised from the dead and sits on the throne of God. They will perish like Terah, the father of Abraham, who refused to go into the promised-land and who was keeping others from entering in. Their unbelieving heart will cause them to be swallowed up like Korah and the sons of Korah. There is but one way out, and only one path, that leads to the promised-land and to the inheritances of God. That is why the warnings are so stern in the book of Hebrews for those who venture to return to the laws of Moses and the legalistic religious systems of this world. The way to the promised-land is not through a system or through a law. It is not directional. You will not be able to find it on a map or on a roadway. The way to the promised-land is a person.

Joshua, the high priest, found this out the hard way as he was called into court for his final sentencing by the judge. Satan had brought a lawsuit against him as the trial before God had been held and put on display before all of heaven. His final sentencing was at hand and his eternity was at stake. The night before he had cold sweats thinking about what would happen to him as he stood before his judge. He was surely guilty of all the charges that Satan had brought against him. There was no doubt about that, and he was deserving of eternal death and separation from God. The cold sweat turned into chills, which left him restless. Joshua's guardian angel that he could not see with his physical eye began to comfort him. It was the same one who would help to escort him into the presence of God upon his death. In the middle of his tossing and turning, Joshua began to receive another revelation in a series of visions that he would have throughout the night.

The first vision was that of Adam. Adam brought before Joshua a pair of fig leaves, the very same ones which he used to cover himself in the garden. They were representative of his efforts to cover his nakedness and sin before a holy and righteous God. The experiment was a miserable failure. When man stands before God, none of his efforts are sufficient to make him righteous before God. Adam spoke of his efforts to hide himself and his sin before a God who was omniscient. The sin of man and the efforts of man brought death and judgment before God. Adam explained to Joshua how Cain had failed in his efforts to be pleasing before God and the sin and judgment that followed because of Cain's insistence on doing things his way. Adam gave Joshua comfort when he spoke of the skins that "GOD HAD PROVIDED" for them. Adam and Eve were not pleasing before God until He Himself had provided for their sins and for them to be righteous before God. There was absolutely nothing that they could do themselves to be made holy, righteous, or godly.

The twisting and turning of Joshua began to subside as he began to reflect on what was said in the court room by the judge himself.[58]

---

[58] Zech 3

A HUDDLE FOR RIGHTEOUSNESS

Joshua knew that the book of Genesis was more than just a book about the lives of four men; Abraham, Isaac, Jacob, and Joseph. He knew that it was a book of blueprints that were set for all of mankind. They were precedents set in stone before the laws of Moses; and that once the die had been cast, that would be the case for quite a time to come. Adam proceeded with his story to Joshua and told him how when God had confronted him in the garden that he not only had tried to hide himself physically by inadequate fig leaves, he tried to hid himself spiritually because his soul was exposed before God. So he hid his sin behind a lie. He had claimed to be afraid when he heard God walking in the garden in the cool of the day. It was a lie and he knew it, and he knew that God knew it. It's an awfully embarrassing thing to be caught in a lie because it reveals our true nature and not only that, it only lasts for a moment before it is exposed and found out.

My seventh grade teacher was a lady by the name of Mrs. Clark. One day and for the first time in her class I spoke of my desire to write a book.

Well, I can still remember that day in September when she had given us math homework to turn in. Everyone was handing in their homework with the exception of the Mulberry kid. The pressure was on as she began going down her class roll and checking to see if everyone had done their assignment. Of course I hadn't, but I was going to do my very best to stall and fake it if necessary. There were a few others before me who had bellied up and just flat out spilled their guts and said that they hadn't done their homework; but not me. I was going to hide behind my fig leaves as long as I could. Well, Mrs. Clark was a veteran of such affairs and had been in this situation at least 10,000 times before I had gotten to her. She knew precisely what to do. Her narrow rimmed glasses had slid down to the brink of her nose but she never once looked up at me. All that she said to me was, "Reggie, where is your homework?"

I hummed and hawed around while squirming in my seat; but I wasn't about to let go of my fig leaves. I said, "I forgot it." I was doing pretty well until the old conscience got the best of me. It was the long silent treatment before her next question that made me sing like a canary. Forgetting was not exactly the best lie that I could tell, but it was the quickest and most convenient lie. It was, however, the next part of the lie that got me in really big trouble and that was when I went down with the ship.

I said, "I left it in my locker!" Now I really didn't need to say that and to add on to the first lie… But once you start lying, it's hard to stop, especially if you get on a roll. You have to tell one lie to cover up the one you just told or forgot about.

Mrs. Clark never looked up and I knew that my goose was cooked. She said while staring at her grade book, "Well, Marsh, go and get it!" Oh Lord my God! I was dead. She really didn't have to put the knife in that far. She could have just let me simmer a little over the fire but, oh no, that was not good enough for Mrs. Clark. She had to embarrass me in front of all of my classmates. Now I have done some extremely dumb things in my life, but this next one I am very proud of. I actually got up out of my chair and went to look for my homework hoping that by some magic that it would all of a sudden pop up. I lingered around and searched through my messy locker knowing that I wasn't about to find my homework. Oh Lord, somebody shoot me! Please shoot me! Anybody! On my way back to the room, I got to thinking just how this was going to look as I walked back into the classroom completely naked and sinful before 40 other kids who know that I had just lied, and told 40 other lies to cover up my previous lie. I thank you so much Adam for fig leaves. They work so wonderfully well. I looked around the corner of my room to see if any of the kids were going to watch me implode as I walked back into the room with my invisible homework. If there had been any other place to run, I would have, believe you me. Yet, Mrs. Clark never looked up when she drove the stake in a little bit deeper. She said, "Marsh, you knew all along that you had never done your homework, so why did you tell me that?"

Oh God! And this was coming from the woman that you gave to me. I was thinking and hiding like Adam. Never again! Not until I knew that I can get away with it for sure the next time.

A HUDDLE FOR RIGHTEOUSNESS

Oh, the fig leaves of Adam simply are not sufficient to cover our nakedness before man let alone before God. So, GOD PROVIDED FOR ADAM AND EVE a covering that would be suitable before him and in his eyes. Adam finished up with his story to Joshua as he told him that God would send a second Adam who would be the skin to cover him and his descendant's.[59] That skin would be the righteousness that would be acceptable before God.

Joshua's mind was beginning to clear and comprehend the righteousness of God but he still had nagging fears and doubts until he saw Abraham with his son Isaac on the altar. What could the sacrifice of Abraham teach him about the righteousness of God? Abraham spoke to Joshua about how he and Sarah could not conceive and have children and how God had to intervene in order for them to have their son Isaac. He told how, through their own efforts and sacrifices, they had almost hijacked God's plan. Then God gave him his final installment plan in his lesson on righteousness. When Abraham took Isaac to the mountains to sacrifice him, God stopped his human sacrifice, and instead of his efforts, he was given a substitute to be sacrificed to God. The substitute would be a stand-in for the sacrifice and offering of Isaac. No human sacrifice was needed to please God. No human effort can suffice to be pleasing to God. God is not looking for our service as much as he is for our hearts. The work had already been done for Abraham; the ram had already been caught in the thicket, the only thing missing was his heart-felt offering before God. Was it righteous before God? And when God saw that Abraham's heart was righteous before him, the angel grabbed his wrist and pointed him to the substitute.

Abraham whispered into Joshua's ear as God had whispered in his ear that all of his human efforts to be a godly priest did not amount to a hill of beans before God. The work to be godly and the work to be righteous had already been done. All that Joshua had to do was walk in them.[60] The fears and sweats of the high priest only then began to subside. Another precedent had been given to

---

[59] John 1:29
[60] Eph 2:8-10

him in light of his sentencing that was coming up before God. His confidence grew even as his time before God approached. What would the judgment be like?

Adam and Abraham had calmed his fears but as he began to enter into the deepest part of his rest, he had his last vision and that was of Moses, the lawgiver. His conversation with Joshua would be the most meaningful of all. The two old men were priests of God and could understand the things of God given unto them through the Holy Scriptures. As they sat face to face and eye to eye, once again the face of Moses began to glow as it did on Mount Sinai, but this time it was different, especially after his meeting with Jesus and Elijah. The fierceness in his eyes had been replaced with tenderness and love for his fellow man, the anger that had originally cost him a trip into the promised-land had been replaced with peace. This Moses was so very different from the old Moses that it struck Joshua's heart very deeply. Moses then began to share the change with Joshua, the high priest. Moses rolled out the scrolls before Joshua and pointed to the verse at the end of the Torah that had escaped him until that very moment. His longer finger pointed, moved along as he read the verse to Joshua. It was the same finger that had condemned the Hebrews for their failure to keep God's laws. Now the finger was pointed back at him. As Moses began to read it aloud to his friend, tears began to stream down his face until he covered his face. As he read, his voice began to tremble when he came to the part that said, "Cursed is everyone that does not keep the whole of the Torah." Joshua began to hear and feel the mistake that Moses had made with the people of God. Both men knew that it was not possible for any man to keep the entire Torah. At the same time that Moses was weeping, Joshua lifted his hands in praise to God and started a prayer of thanksgiving that God had set him free. God never intended for men to try and keep the Holy Scriptures[61]. Man had not been made for the Sabbath; but the Sabbath had been made for man. Men were made for relationships with God not for the keeping of laws and regulations; *for the righteous man shall live by faith*

---

[61] Rom 5:20, Gal 3:10-11

alone.[62] Righteousness is not in the keeping of a set of standards or in the trying to live for God, because for every standard, principle, and scripture obeyed, there are ten thousand others that we have broken or will break.[63]

The chains had fallen off Joshua as the vision began to fade away with his dreams. His sleep was sweet from that point on as the tossing and the turning ceased. The next day Joshua would be able to face his judgment with confidence. His guardian angel looked on his assignment with a knowing smile on his face, for he was but a ministering spirit who had been sent by God to help him in his journey on earth. He sighed as the old man lay quietly on his bed and began to snore loudly. The guardian angel was privileged to watch the redemption of man.

The next day Joshua entered the courtroom to face the judgment of God. There was light! Tremendous blinding light, which only celestial beings, could bear to stand. Joshua shielded his eyes as he approached the throne of God. A powerful voice spoke to him which sounded like the force of a million gallons of water rushing down the side of the mountains. It shook Joshua to the core such as nothing had ever shaken him before. The light was full of the brilliant colors of the rainbow as the form on the throne was transparent. The 'light' spoke again and Joshua buckled at the knees. A powerful hand lifted him to his feet and raised his chin to see the form on the throne of God. The form had changed before him instantly and what he saw this time amazed him to the point of tears. He saw a lamb sitting in the middle of the throne. It was a lamb that had the look of one that had been slain. The form changed again before his very eyes and this time the form became that of a man who had scars in his hands and on his feet. As he ventured to approach the throne, he began to gaze at the man and was invited to move closer to take a better look. To his amazement, the figure was that of his old defense attorney; the one who had defended him against the lawsuit that had been brought to court by Satan. Joshua had never noticed the scars

---

[62] Gal 3:11
[63] James 2:10

until now, for they had been covered beneath his robe. He fell to his knees in worship and in praise. Satan, the prosecutor who was shamefully disgusted with this entire scene, asked that the evidence against Joshua be repeated to him. The bailiff, who was very helpful and nice (much better than the one that I had) went to get the records on Joshua and could not find any recorded sin against him. "Why?" he screamed. "Why aren't there any records of Joshua's sin?" The judge rose from the throne and all of heaven was silent. He showed the prosecuting attorney his wounds and his scars and said to him, I have paid the debt for Joshua and I, alone, am also his redemption and his righteousness. Satan left the court room and went out with a vengeance to try and find someone else that he could deceive. God had imputed his righteousness and his nature to all who would believe in him[64] and had charged no one with their sins.[65] The judge then called for a robe to be brought to Joshua; brand new robe that represented the righteousness of God. It was brilliant like the sun shining in its strength. There was no giant screen in heaven showing all of his sins before the entire universe. There was no record of him punching the lights out of old fat Sanballat when he was harassing him at the building of the temple. There was none of that. There was no need to bring up something that was in the past and had already been paid for. For a moment, as Joshua looked at his attorney and judge, he saw the same eyes of compassion that the woman caught in adultery saw, and he was asked the same question. "Where are your accusers?" And the response was; "there is none here Lord."

Rev. Blanton had told me once that all of my sins were going to be displayed on a big screen in heaven for all the citizens of heaven to watch in shame and that Jesus was going to give me a royal chewing out and take away my wings. Apparently, he must have felt that way after he had eaten all of our chickens and their wings because I sure can't find that in the scripture. *Why in the world would Jesus spend*

---

[64] 2Peter 1:4
[65] Psalm 32:1-2

time rehearsing all of my bad deeds when he has dealt with them; would it be just for old time' sake? I don't think so.

Now if Rev. Blanton wants to have all of his sins blown up on a huge screen, we will be more than happy to bring in the popcorn, cookies, and cokes, all three of us; just as long as his wife does not play the piano. All that the screen would show would be him eating up everybody's chickens.

Joshua's verdict was handed down long before he stood before the judgment seat of God. His mind raced back to the vision of the man in the temple sitting upon the Holy of Holies between the Cherubim. No man ever sits upon the Holy of Holies between the two angels and lives to tell about it. This is why they have a rope tied to one of the legs on the priests so that when they screw up, they can pull them out; because no one in his right mind is going to go in after any of them. When you sit down in the Holy of Holies, it means that your work in the temple is finished and completed and that there is no more to be done. Priests never sat down in the temple because their work was never done. So why was this man sitting where only God could sit? Then Joshua realized that the man that he saw on the judgment throne of God was one and the same with the one sitting down in the temple. God's priestly duties had been done. He had atoned for the sins of man; he had reconciled the world back to God; and he had become the righteousness of man before God. Now seeing that men who believe are in Christ and Christ is in them, God is not terribly excited about judging himself and that is what he would have to do to judge the man who believes in Jesus Christ alone for salvation. Jesus Christ is our righteousness.[66]

In the midst of Joshua's judgment, something magnificent began to transpire. The white robe that had been awarded to him for his faithfulness began to glow and glow. With each change of light the robe became whiter and whiter and Joshua's joy kept increasing the more the robe changed and the brighter it got. His knowledge of God increased with each illumination of light until his joy was full. When his judgment was over, Joshua was radiant from head to toe

---

[66] 1Cor 1:30

and his love of Jesus Christ grew more and more. The knowledge that he now possessed was unequalled by anything that the earth had ever produced. He had complete knowledge of the beings around him and the creation around him and there was no contamination in his knowledge. It was perfect and lacking in nothing whatsoever. Adam had possessed a small portion of it before the fall but now Joshua possessed knowledge in its most perfect form. His skin glowed beneath his shiny new white robe. And when he approached the saints, it was like watching the sunrise on a cloudless morning. God had made all things beautiful in its time. Now not all of the priests of God and not all of the people of God shone as brightly as Joshua did. Not all of God's people received the same reward for their priestly service.

I wondered who some of those preachers and pastors could be! Hmmm! That could be a hard one if you didn't live in Mulberry. Could it be someone we all know? I would be willing to throw in a couple of third grade teachers that I once knew.

Now once the believer has received his reward, he is stuck with it for all eternity, that's it. And just as there are levels of bliss in heaven, there are also levels of agony in hell, and the unbeliever is stuck forever in his permanent state. Joshua's body was changed from mortality to immortality in a moment. It was indestructible and eternal. It bore none of the scars that he had on this earth either physically or emotionally. The old memories that tormented him were a thing of the past because he had received a new mind that was perfect in righteousness and holiness and the body that he once had no longer suffered ills nor could it ever be damaged again. It could take him to his destination in an instant. It could also go through any wall or any surface in heaven or on the face of the earth. When Joshua looked up at the bluest sky he had ever seen, he noticed that there was no sun and no moon.

Chapter Fourteen

This was the place that Ronnie and I had dreamed about and talked about as we were lying on our backs in the middle of the tall grass while gathering ticks on our butts. We knew that somewhere over the rainbow there was a place like this but our earthly mind could not fathom it. We could imagine a body that never needed food or water and never grew tired. With that kind of body we could play basketball all day and every Sunday afternoon until we dropped. We could imagine an earth populated with people of good will and a government that ran properly because the leaders ruled with a rod of iron. It would be a perfect place with no night and no darkness as there would be no end to the kingdom of God.

What Ronnie and I could not see in our mind's eye however, was the shining city of gold coming down out of the heavens like a beautiful bride having been adorned for her husband. It descended at a very slow pace as it sparkled and glistened in the heavens. In it the streets were paved with gold and there were twelve gates with the names of twelve apostles on them. On the outskirts of the city were trees bearing all kinds of fruits for the healing of the nations. Inside of this magnificent city that stretched from Maine to Texas in length, height, and width, were many mansions adorned with precious metals and jewels. The mansions were of different sizes and in different shapes, but the city itself was a perfect square. We felt a twinge of sadness because at the gates of this city there were angels to let in those for whom the city had been prepared and to keep out those for whom the city had not been prepared. The city was huge enough to accommodate billions and billions of God's people. There were men and angels going to and fro in and out of the city all dressed in robes of different colors and sizes. Men and women wore great smiles of joy at meeting each other seeing that there were no flaws in them. Each time they met it was as if it was the very first time. In the center of the city was this huge banquet hall that was constantly filled with the guests of the King. Those who stood on the outside of the hall could only watch and wonder what it was like to be inside feasting with the King of Kings. Yes, there were those who were not allowed to come into the banquet hall and to eat even though they possessed eternal life and would live forever. They could only watch from a distance. Every one inside the hall had on robes of righteousness that had been provided to them by the King as they feasted to their hearts desire. Those who populated the earth and had entered the millennium had access to heaven but not to the eternal city. They would share life on earth but no mansion had been prepared for them.

Now Joshua's reward was great in heaven but he also had a reward that was waiting for him on the earth; the redeemed earth that was now populated with billions and billions of people. For his faithfulness, God had made him the priest and king over ten cities here on earth; where he would rule with a rod of iron. I told my friend Ronnie that if God ever made me ruler over ten cities that I would be taking dips in Hawaii. We laughed until we were silly thinking of how it would be. Wherever it would be, I would be happy as long as I had a crack at Mrs. Platt, my third grade teacher. I would definitely assign her homework for ten years running and make her to play every instrument that she had never seen in her lifetime. She would never be able to dress in red again, but would have to wear long black dresses with a veil over her face; and if she ever took it off, I would whack her hands with a stick the way she did me in the third grade. We laughed at our silly thoughts of heaven as we choked on that green old sour dot weed. We knew there would be none of that in heaven but I sure would plead with the Lord for a crack at those two policemen who gave me tickets. If they ever ended up under my jurisdiction in heaven, they might just want to consider going to the other place.

Life in heaven is not the same as we picture it here on earth. There are no angels and people flying around playing a harp every day. That is not heaven at all. Heaven has eternal life for all who go there with the absence of sin. Heaven is uninterrupted joy. Heaven has judges and rulers who rule over nations, cities, and towns. There are administrative duties to perform in heaven. There are judges who will still have to govern the lives of people who are living on earth for all eternity.[67] Yes, they are perfect; yes, they are sinless, but they are still human beings living on earth that have to be governed. Do not be surprised to hear someone mutter to you that this place looks somewhat vaguely familiar.

Now somewhere in one of the blackest holes ever created is a monument to the will of men. It is a place that I'd rather not talk about and will venture not to linger too long here. This place was never created for mankind but for Satan and his angels.[68] It was never meant to be a dwelling place for men but some who do not enjoy the presence of God are sent to a place of their choosing. God sends them there to accommodate their own desires. He has no other place to send them. In his presence their torment would be much greater than hell because of their hatred and disbelief in him, so he allows them where they are free from his presence. This is the place that Ronnie and I feared the most and the place that my Aunt Ruby described. *It is a place*. It is not a figment of my imagination. *It is real*.

On the other hand, God has prepared a perfect place called the New Jerusalem. There is a river that runs through the center of it that is never polluted and its water is crystal clear. On each side of the river you will find the trees of life, which bare all manner of fruits and yields its fruit twelve months out of the year. And its leaves are for the healing of the nations. The garden that was destroyed because of Adam has been restored and once again God reigns over his kingdom of righteousness.

---

[67] Rev 20:4
[68] Matt 25:41

EPILOGUE

Ronnie and I were stretched out in the midst of the tall Johnson grass and Bermuda infested weeds as we began to think about how heaven was and what it would be like. As we lay with our hands locked behind our heads and ever ready to swat at horseflies, ants, and chiggers that had grown deeply interested as to why we were laying right smack dab in the center of their territory. The blue and white fluffies overhead seemed to take on different forms and we entered into silence and long periods of meditation. In my minds eye I could see Abel who was slain by his brother Cain with a great look of joy on his face as he had overcome. However, Cain was not to be seen. Other faces began to pop next to Abel as the witnesses kept increasing. There was Abraham the father of faith along with Sarah who was called out of Ur of the Chaldees into the promise land of Canaan.

God had given them all new names to fit their righteous character along with long white robes of righteousness. The new names represented more than their character is also represented the number of trials that they had overcome while here on earth.

The crowd continued to grow larger and larger with everyone wearing long white robes of righteousness that varied in different shades of brightness which was symbolic of their rewards received.

By now the huge crowd had emerged into this massive huddle of thousands and thousands of people surrounding me cheering me on in my walk with Jesus Christ. I think the most surprising face of all in this huddle was that of Rahab. *RAHAB WAS A PROSTITUTE.* Why in the world would a *prostitute* be in the middle of this huddle of righteous people? Her robe of righteousness was just as bright as the others and the smile on her face was just as large. There were no kept records of the past and no knowledge of the past.

God had made everything new and they had all surrounded me as a cloud of witnesses[69] to encourage me in my walk with Christ.

They are watching over us as we overcome every obstacle placed in our path and at our door. They were there to remind me that they had gone before and overcome. THEY WERE RIGHTEOUS BEFORE GOD!

---

[69] Hebrews 11, 12:1

EDITORIAL

The prophet Zechariah is responsible for the writing of, "A Huddle for Righteousness." More specifically the vision that God gave to him in Chapter 3:1-5. This hit me like a ton of bricks as I was trying to come to grips with living a life that is pleasing and righteous before a holy and living God and was failing miserably at it.

Joshua the High Priest was seen standing before God due to a lawsuit that had been brought on him by Satan the evil one. The garments that he wore that day before God were filthy and dirty which was symbolic of his sins and unrighteousness. Satan had the goods on Joshua like a cat burglar loaded with precious diamonds. Joshua was as guilty as sin; pardon the pun. There was no denying the charges against him, no ifs ands or buts about it; he could not pass go or collect 200 dollars; he was guilty with a period after it.

That is when God stepped to remedy the situation and to cut short the accusations, the condemnations, the guilt, the shame, and a million other things that come with being found guilty before God. His voice struck like lightning from the sky when he said,

"The Lord rebukes you O Satan! Even the Lord who has chosen Jerusalem rebukes you. Is this not a brand that has been plucked from the fire? With one single statement of rebuttal God silenced all of heaven against Joshua." [70]

Well after picking myself up off the floor, I began reading the scriptures in a different light as I noticed that there was a common theme such as with Joshua that ran all throughout the scriptures beginning with Genesis and ending with the book of the Revelation. It started when God gave Adam and Eve skins to cover their nakedness

---

[70] Zech 3:1-5

and ended with the Revelation with the saints receiving white garments of the righteousness of God. This kind of righteousness had been given to the people of God; it was not earned in any way shape or form.

As I began to ponder the scriptures, I then realized that the reformer Martin Luther had a very similar experience when he was reading the very first chapter of Romans. He too was embroiled in a religious system that was corrupt to the core and God wanted there to be some changes. As he was reading verse 17, it dawned on him that the religions of that day were requiring of men to perform for their salvation and to be pleasing to God. These corrupt practices of the church were keeping men and women from entering the kingdom of God and his righteousness. They had been selling indulgences for the forgiveness of their sins in much the same way as we pay tithes and offerings to rebuke the devourer.

After bouncing checks to pay my tithes, a great man of God asked me a very specific and direct question concerning the practices of my church. He asked me "Why was I allowing my pastor to put me under the law of God rather than the grace of God?" GOOD QUESTION! I had been too busy to really give it any thought; all I wanted to be was pleasing to God; and the pastors are men of God. So, as a result I should be obedient to what they are telling me about the things of God.

It was the continuous jumping through the hoops of the dos and don'ts of the local church, church doctrine and teachings that finally did me in. I finally said, "This is not working and I quit." That is when the change started in me.

The second reason that I am writing this book is because of my neighbor across the street. He is not a religious man that I know of, but he does not want to hear about or even be close to anything that is remotely Christian or about God. Now that is very odd because his brother is a very devout Christian who shuts down his medical practice on Friday 6:00 p.m. and reopens on Monday in strict observance of the Sabbath. If he makes any money during this time it goes directly to his church. So, why is it that his own flesh and blood who admires his convictions cannot stand the things of God?

The final reason for the writing of this book is the degree of spiritual blindness in this country due to organized religion and ignorance of the things of God. I originally thought that spiritual blindness was an issue that unbelievers had to deal with but I have come to realize that it is just as prevalent among Christians.

About the Book

There are so many believers out there who have fallen through the cracks. They love the Lord Jesus Christ with all of their hearts but they are fed up with organized religion. They have seen through the masks that are being worn today and they will have absolutely nothing to do with it and *I do not blame them one bit.*

Many, who are not only spiritually blind but also politically blind, believe that the kingdom of God and his righteousness will arrive on the backs of donkeys and elephants or fly in on Air Force One. Not so! Not in this life or the life to come will that happen. The kingdom of God will come when God set it in motion in the fullness of his time and not necessarily in our time.

A lot of Christians are praying and fasting to twist the arms of God until He takes up their agenda when the real truth is that we have to find out what God's agenda is and where He is raining down His blessings; go and find that cloud and get wet!

About the Author

1971 was a good year for Reggie White. He was one of two Afro-American boys chosen to receive an Athletic Scholarship from the University of Arkansas where he decided to study Business Education – "Out of confusion," he said. "I didn't know whether I wanted to be a teacher or a businessman."

He studied hard, applied himself but something became apparent in his second and third year of university – Reggie White had talent; he was a very good football player. Amongst the people who noticed his ability to play ball were the owners of the New York Giants. They didn't wait until he finished college to pick him up to play his first season in 1975.

During the four years that Reggie spent with the Giants, in his spare time, he didn't go to the discos or the clubs; no – he roamed the streets of New York in discontent. He was looking for something else than fame and fortune which he had suddenly acquired. He was looking for companionship out of his loneliness. That's when he started walking in-step with the ultimate guide – Jesus Christ. He was not 'a pillar of the church' by any means nor was he even a 'church goer' – he was just a man in search of the truth that responded to his destiny.

Three years on, the Detroit Lions wanted Reggie and they traded for him. Reggie accepted the decision and moved to Detroit. All the while making sure that his every stride was in keeping with the Lord. During this period, the first extraordinary event occurred – not a miracle; just the first in a long line of decisions that Reggie was to make. He decided to fast, as Jesus did, for forty days and forty nights. Silly isn't it? Not so, when you think of why Reggie did such a thing. He wanted to feel what Jesus felt, he wanted to meet his mentor half-way at least and comprehend his teachings to the fullest.

Through that first year with the Lions, Reggie sustained terrible injuries which retired him for awhile. While he recuperated after numerous surgeries, he went back to college and finished his degree in 'Business Education'. That gave him the knowledge to 'teach' people and youngsters. However, for Reggie, life was far from complete; he was not satisfied. He needed something else. By then he had a career awaiting him, a house, money in the bank and a bright future ahead of him. But instead of returning to the world of football, even as a coach, what does he do? He watches a program on television that tells him of the miseries of this world and decides that it is time for him to count his blessings and to chuck everything away. He sells his house, gives away all of his belongings, shuts the door on the lot and decides to walk his life 'by faith' alone. Why on earth would anyone in their right mind do that? Again – Reggie needed to walk in Jesus footsteps.

He is literally homeless now; he gets a job here and there and lives on alms – *of his own volition!* From that point on, Reggie is no longer the venerated football player that he was; he is *the missionary that he wants to be.*

Yet Reggie soon realizes that he needs to learn, and become a teacher of the word of God. So, he goes to the Dallas Theological Seminary where he acquires his Masters Degree in Theology over a period of six years during which time he decides to get coaching or teaching jobs where ever he can, to save money and to put pen to paper.

His first book is still in the closet; but the second one has a message – finally Reggie knows what his destiny has in reserve for him. He is a messenger of Jesus; not a prophet, not a preacher, just *a messenger* who has lived life on both sides of the fence.

He has discovered what a 'huddle for righteousness' means and he tells the reader about his findings in the most entertaining way.

"It makes for an intriguing and pleasurable read..."

Printed in the United States
39573LVS00004B/65